Epperson v. Arkansas:
The Evolution–Creationism Debate

Jonathan L. Thorndike

Landmark Supreme Court Cases

Enslow Publishers, Inc.

44 Fadem Road   PO Box 38
Box 699   Aldershot
Springfield, NJ 07081   Hants GU12 6BP
USA   UK
http://www.enslow.com

Library of Congress Cataloging-in-Publication Data

Thorndike, Jonathan L., 1959–
    Epperson v. Arkansas: the evolution–creationism debate /
Jonathan L. Thorndike.
        p. cm. — (Landmark Supreme Court cases)
    Includes bibliographical references and index.
    Summary: Examines the 1968 Supreme Court case that dealt with the question
of whether teaching creationism rather than evolution in schools in Arkansas was
acceptable.
        ISBN 0-7660-1084-8
        1. Epperson, Susan—Trials, litigation, etc.—Juvenile literature. 2. Arkansas—Trials,
litigation, etc.—Juvenile literature. 3. Evolution—Study and teaching—Law and
legislation —Arkansas—Juvenile literature. 4. Evolution—Study and teaching—
Law and legislation—United States—Juvenile literature. [1.Epperson, Susan—Trials,
litigation, etc. 2. Arkansas—Trials, litigation, etc. 3. Evolution.] I. Title. II. Series.
KF224.E66T48   1999
345.767'0288—dc21   98-21605
                                                                CIP
                                                                 AC

Printed in the United States of America.

10 9 8 7 6 5 4 3 2 1

Photo Credits: *Arkansas Democrat Gazette,* pp. 46, 51, 56, 58, 64, 66, 67, 75;
Courtesy of the Little Rock, Arkansas, Chamber of Commerce, p. 38; Corel
Corporation, p. 42; Harris and Ewing, Collection of the Supreme Court of the
United States, p. 89; Hessler Studios, Collection of the Supreme Court of the
United States, p. 95; *The Origins of Species,* p. 18; Reproduced from the Collections
of the Library of Congress, pp. 11, 14, 21, 26, 30, 109, 115.

Cover Photo: Courtesy of the Little Rock, Arkansas, Chamber of Commerce.

Contents

Acknowledgments

Many people helped with the research and writing of this book. The librarians at Lakeland College and the Mead Public Library in Sheboygan, Wisconsin, were very good at locating the unusual materials needed for primary research. Katherine Van Sluys and Amy Anderson provided professional, detailed copyediting suggestions. Claudia Thorndike also read the whole manuscript several times and provided needed support and encouragement. The author is grateful and owes many thanks to these people and unnamed others for their assistance.

1

Susan Epperson's Dilemma

Susan Epperson was a biology teacher in Arkansas in 1965. She and her school would become the focus of a national debate and a Supreme Court ruling about theories of the origins of human beings.

How did human beings come into this world? Did God create man and woman (creationism), as told in the first book of the Bible, or did humans evolve from apes (evolution)? Many scientists support the theory of evolution, while many Christians believe in the Creation theory as presented in the Bible. How did evolution and creationism play into a United States Supreme Court case involving a high school biology teacher in Arkansas?

Charles Darwin's Theory

In 1859, British scientist Charles Darwin used the word "evolution" to describe the theory of the gradual development of the earth's animal and plant life. Darwin wrote about a very slow process of change that took generations to achieve noticeable results. Evolution, according to Darwin, is how animal and plant species adapted to changing environmental conditions— changes in the earth's climate, availability of food, and competition from predators or other animals.

Scientists who accept Darwin's view of evolution support their reasoning by finding rocks with embedded fossil evidence of various plants and animals that have changed forms over time or become extinct. These scientists believe the truth is found solely through observing, reasoning, finding evidence, and testing theories. Creationists believe the truth is revealed primarily through the Bible.

Fundamentalist Views

During the time of the United States Supreme Court case *Epperson v. Arkansas* in 1968, the Christians opposed to Darwin's theory had not made much use of the word "creationist" yet. Instead, they called themselves fundamentalists, people who believe in the literal truth of the Bible. They argue that God created the animals, plants, and humans, according to the order laid out in Genesis, the first book of the Bible. Daylight was created on the first day; the sky was created on the second day; water, land, and plants were created on the third day; sun, moon, and stars were created on the fourth day; sea creatures, birds, and fish were created on the fifth day; cattle, wildlife, reptiles, and people were created on the sixth day.[1]

Creationism

Creationism describes a biblical theory of how plants and animals came to their current forms. Instead of using the word "creationism," those who believe God created all life on earth may also describe their view as "intelligent design theory" or "abrupt appearance theory."[2] Supporters of creationism and "Creation Scientists"—who sometimes have serious scientific training and sometimes have backgrounds in religion— believe the Christian God created Earth within the six-day period described in Genesis. Some creationists believe Earth is only six thousand years old and that each of the six days of creation mentioned in Genesis was exactly twenty-four hours long.[3]

Creationists cite the biblical story in Genesis as evidence for this time frame and challenge the authenticity of fossils. They argue that Darwin's theory was not observed by any people and that the fossil record is lacking some essential transition species that would prove a link between human beings and apelike ancestors. Creationists believe the truth is based on revelation of God's purpose as it was revealed long ago to the writers of the Bible.

Evolution versus Creationism

The fight between evolution and creationism raises many complex issues of religious belief, separation of government and religion, freedom of speech, government control of school curriculum, and academic freedom of teachers to teach and students to learn. This debate continues in some school districts across the United States. At its center is the idea that human life would seem less important if not created by a divine authority. Creationists believe that humans could not have evolved from animals. They believe that an all-powerful supreme being must have authorized and controlled the purpose of Creation. All the life forms on Earth, including man and woman, owe their existence to God's creation of life. God created humans in his own image, unlike animals, which some Christians believe do not have souls.

Historical Overview and School Curriculum

During the nineteenth century, many people tried to balance the competing claims of evolution and creationism. People said that evolution was science and creationism was religion. These separate but equally important subjects did not need to interfere with each other. But in the twentieth century, many court cases and legal actions upset the balance, as one side of the debate tried to tip the balance in its favor. Often, legal actions focused on school curriculum. What should children learn? Creationists often pressured local school boards to adopt textbooks sympathetic to their views. Scientists wanted Darwin's theory to be taught in biology class because it is the most widely accepted theory of how different species adapt to change. Creationists wanted the story of Creation in Genesis to be taught in biology class. After all, it explained how life began, and the United States was historically linked with Christianity. Many early immigrant groups came to the United States because they were persecuted Christians; immigrants came from European countries to the United States because they wanted to practice their religion freely.

The *Scopes* Trial

Before Susan Epperson, people were already familiar with the evolution and creationism arguments. One of the most celebrated trials in American history involved evolution and creationism. In 1925, a lower court in Dayton, Tennessee, convicted and fined science teacher John T. Scopes one hundred dollars for teaching Darwin's theory of evolution to his class. At that time, Tennessee state law made it illegal for teachers to teach anything other than a strictly literal biblical view of human creation. The country's best-known criminal lawyer, Clarence Darrow, defended Scopes. The famous, fiery politician William Jennings Bryan assisted in the prosecution.[4] Bryan and the prosecutors argued that Scopes violated Tennessee law by teaching evolution. This theory claimed humans evolved from earlier primates or an apelike relative.

The nation had its eyes and ears fixed upon the outcome of this trial. Newspaper reporters and a curious public crowded into the courtroom to listen to the arguments. The *Scopes* trial developed a circuslike atmosphere. This came about in part because of sensational accounts written by newspaper reporters, who labeled it the "Monkey Trial." When Bryan took the stand as a Bible expert and allowed Darrow to cross-examine him, the trial reached its turning point. Bryan argued for a moral, symbolic truth in the Bible. Darrow tried to pin Bryan down on the literal meaning of his testimony:

Darrow: "Upon thy belly thou shalt go, and dust shalt

Clarence Darrow was the lawyer who defended John T. Scopes in the 1925 *Scopes* trial that lead the way for Susan Epperson's case.

thou eat all the days of thy life." Do you think that is why the serpent is compelled to crawl upon its belly?

Bryan: I believe that.

Darrow: Have you any idea how the snake went before that time?

Bryan: No, sir.

Darrow: Do you know whether he walked on his tail or not?

Bryan: No, sir, I have no way to know. [Laughter][5]

Bryan dueled with Darrow, a master of cross-examination, as Darrow attempted to humiliate Bryan by challenging his biblical literalism. Bryan fell into Darrow's carefully designed logical trap. The razor-sharp intellect of Darrow forced Bryan into admitting that the six consecutive, twenty-four-hour periods he affirmed as the biblical truth of Creation must be incorrect. Darrow outsmarted Bryan into confessing that the Genesis story of Creation must have taken longer than just six days, even though Bryan was there to defend the Tennessee law and the Bible. Darrow also got Bryan to indirectly admit that Christians had no real case to argue against Darwin.[6] Darrow argued for the scientific validity of evolution and against the constitutionality of the Tennessee law. However, he did not deny that Scopes had broken the law. Scopes was convicted and fined one hundred dollars despite Darrow's defense against Bryan.

Two weeks later, Bryan collapsed and died of a heart

attack. He had won the trial but lost his life in this high-stakes battle for the nation's conscience. The Tennessee State Supreme Court later reversed the conviction of John T. Scopes. The Tennessee law forbidding the teaching of Darwin's theory remained on the books, however, until 1967. Laws against the teaching of evolution in other states were unchallenged in the United States Supreme Court until Susan Epperson came along.[7] Susan Epperson began her fight against Arkansas's antievolution law in 1965, some forty years after John T. Scopes's conviction.

After the *Scopes* Trial

Following the *Scopes* trial in 1925, twenty southern states rushed to pass antievolution laws.[8] These states were mostly in the southeastern part of the United States, between Georgia and Texas. Evangelical Protestant churches such as the Baptists and Methodists had been the most successful at spreading religion in the South. These churches emphasized a literal reading of the Bible, believing that God created all life on Earth in six twenty-four-hour periods, and then God stopped. Evangelicals claim evolution is impossible. God created everything on Earth, in the seas, and in the skies, and then He rested. No living creature changed form after God created it, according to these Christians. In

Famous politician William Jennings Bryan and the prosecution in the *Scopes* trial argued that John T. Scopes violated Tennessee law by teaching evolution. Bryan won his case but died two weeks later of a heart attack.

Arkansas, a group known as the American Anti-evolution Association, headed by the Reverend Ben Bogard, wanted to make a statement. Bogard persuaded the state lawmakers to adopt a law in 1928. It expressly forbade any state-supported school or university "to teach the theory or doctrine that mankind ascended or descended from a lower order of animals."[9]

Arkansas Law Neither Enforced nor Challenged

For nearly forty years, the Arkansas law was neither enforced nor challenged. When adopted in 1928, the law represented the views of certain fundamentalist Christians who believed in a literal interpretation of the Bible. Many other citizens of Arkansas wanted full consideration of all branches of science in their schools.

In 1965, when Susan Epperson began teaching, science teachers in cities like Little Rock and Fayetteville, Arkansas, had been teaching evolution for years. (Just four years later, in 1969, the first manned space mission would successfully land on the moon.) Teachers did not know the law against it even existed. Meanwhile in small towns and rural areas, evolution was never mentioned by teachers. Educators avoided teaching the theory of evolution outside of larger cities in Arkansas. But if teachers did mention evolution, they were not prosecuted as criminals. Because it was not enforced, the law became only a reminder of an earlier time. With the exception of a few outspoken religious people in rural areas of the state, most people did not really support the antievolution law.

Putting the Law to the Test

Many educators in Arkansas wanted to test the 1928 law. Did people still feel so strongly against Darwin and for the Bible? Were the feelings of Arkansas's teachers, parents, ministers, and students as strong in 1965 as they were during the famous *Scopes* "Monkey Trial?"

Susan Epperson was about to find out. Little Rock's Central High School was about to become a battleground.

Teachers' freedom to teach and students' freedom to learn were big issues. Many years had passed since 1928, and people were now more accepting of different theories about the creation of life on Earth. Many teachers felt that the antievolution law denied them their First Amendment right of freedom of speech. They felt that by allowing the law to exist, Arkansas supported an official religion (Christianity). This was in violation of the Constitution, which states that "Congress shall make no law respecting an establishment of religion, or prohibiting the free exercise thereof." The Arkansas Education Association (AEA) and its attorney, Eugene Warren, searched for a test case to prevent the state from enforcing its antievolution law. Eugene Warren believed that science teachers "always had a cloud over their heads" because state law forbade discussion of Darwin's theory of evolution.[10]

Susan Epperson Steps Up

Susan Epperson was a perfect teacher for the Arkansas State Education Association to approach about challenging the outdated law. Her mother and father had raised her in the Presbyterian Church, a traditional Christian Protestant denomination. Prosecuting lawyers could not accuse her of being an atheist, someone who does not believe in God. Moreover, Susan Epperson's father taught biology at the College of the Ozarks in Arkansas. It was a Christian college for rural students who did not have much money. Susan attended Arkansas public schools and the College of the Ozarks. Prosecutors would not be able to portray her as an outsider meddling in Arkansas's affairs. Epperson's husband served as a lieutenant in the United States Air Force, with top security clearance. Prosecutors could not accuse her of Communist sympathies.[11] (Many people feared Communists during the 1960s because they believed the Communists and the Soviet Union plotted to take over all world governments.)

Yet the decision to challenge the law was not easy. Susan Epperson faced a dilemma. The tenth-grade teacher reviewed her school district's newly adopted, official textbook. She found a chapter on Darwin's theory of evolution. That would not surprise most science teachers; Charles Darwin first published his theory of evolution in 1859 in a book entitled *On the Origin of Species by Means of Natural Selection*. Yet Epperson risked losing her job if she so much as mentioned Darwin's theory to her class.[12]

ON

THE ORIGIN OF SPECIES

BY MEANS OF NATURAL SELECTION,

OR THE

PRESERVATION OF FAVOURED RACES IN THE STRUGGLE FOR LIFE.

By CHARLES DARWIN, M.A.,

FELLOW OF THE ROYAL, GEOLOGICAL, LINNÆAN, ETC., SOCIETIES;
AUTHOR OF 'JOURNAL OF RESEARCHES DURING H. M. S. BEAGLE'S VOYAGE
ROUND THE WORLD.'

LONDON:

JOHN MURRAY, ALBEMARLE STREET.

1859.

The right of Translation is reserved.

Charles Darwin first published his theory of evolution in 1859 in his book entitled *On the Origins of Species by Means of Natural Selection.*

The Arkansas law "prohibited the teaching in its public schools and universities of the theory that man evolved from other species of life."[13] The law made it illegal for a teacher in any state-supported school or university "to teach the theory or doctrine that mankind ascended or descended from a lower order of animals" or "to adopt or use in any such institution a textbook that teaches" this theory.[14] Until 1965, the official textbook furnished for high school biology did not have a chapter on evolution. The Little Rock teachers and administrators who selected a new biology textbook with a chapter on Darwin's theory of evolution were simply unaware of the law. It had never been enforced. It had been forty years since people in Arkansas were really angry about Darwin's theory. Violators were subject to loss of employment and a fine of up to five hundred dollars. Arkansas never prosecuted anyone for violating the law, however. Many communities ignored the law, not even aware of its existence. This was because the *Scopes* trial and the 1928 law were in the distant past. Arkansas had changed a lot since 1928. Not many people knew about the law, not even teachers and members of school boards.

For the academic year 1965–66, teachers of biology in the Little Rock school system recommended and adopted a new textbook that contained a chapter setting forth the theory about the origin of man from a lower order of animal.[15] Should Susan Epperson teach the chapter about Darwin from the official textbook? Scientists considered Darwin's theory of natural selection and evolution a mainstream, working theory about how biological species adapt to environments and change over time.

Like John T. Scopes, Susan Epperson was twenty-four years old when she challenged the law. Central High School in Little Rock had hired Epperson only recently, in the fall of 1964. Epperson's job obligated her to instruct her students in accepted theories of science. With only one year of teaching experience, Epperson wondered if she should teach the officially adopted text and its chapter about evolution, thus breaking the law.

It was a no-win situation. If Epperson chose to teach the chapter, she violated a state law. She was subject to a five hundred dollar fine and dismissal from her job. But if Epperson chose to ignore the chapter, she violated the terms of her employment by the Little Rock school system. It had hired her to teach *all* branches of biology and accepted theories about how life evolved on Earth. Epperson could violate the terms of her teaching contract (and not teach evolution) or go against state law and teach Darwin's theory. Whatever she chose

Susan Epperson holds the textbook that violated the antievolution law.

to do, Epperson would break either the law or some guidelines of professional conduct.

In the minds of many people, the case of *Epperson* v. *Arkansas* looked easy to settle. Why would state law prevent a teacher from teaching? Yet the controversy was far from simple. The *Epperson* case would be the first ruling by the United States Supreme Court on this issue. However, school districts across America continue today to fight this same battle. The creationists, as they came to be known, would invent new strategies to cut Darwin out of the school curriculum. In his book *Under God: Religion and American Politics,* Garry Wills wrote that the biblical account of Creation "is not going to go away as a political issue, for the obvious cultural reason that the Bible is not going to stop being the central book in our intellectual heritage."[16]

So Susan Epperson was about to step into a court-room battle that would attempt to resolve this old conflict between science and religion. Before describing the two sides getting ready for the fight, let us step back in history and look at the beginning of the ideas that led to Susan Epperson's battle.

2

Two Theories Behind the Conflict

The British scientist Charles Darwin, whose writings created the controversy in the *Epperson* case, at first trained to be a minister in the Church of England. Darwin was uncertain about pursuing a career in the church, however, and he was very interested in the world of nature. In part to delay his decision about starting a job with the Church of England, Darwin worked aboard the English government ship *Beagle* on a scientific exploration around South America from 1831 through 1836.[1]

Darwin's Scientific Observations

On the trip, Darwin observed and catalogued the tremendous varieties of birds, land animals, and plants found on remote islands. He noted the differences between those animals on islands and those found on the mainland. He especially noticed the varieties of the animals' markings, coloration, size, shape, internal organs, limbs, and behavior. These observations led Darwin to believe that animals are changed by their interaction with the environment. Darwin did not know what the differences in size and coloring of animals were attributed to. Perhaps they resulted from chance happenings in nature. Perhaps they were the result of the animals' adaptations to living on different islands far removed from the mainland.

The Theory of Natural Selection

After much research, Darwin theorized that physical differences between species might be caused by what he termed natural selection. Natural selection refers to a complex, interactive process among plants, animals, and habitats. It takes place over a long period of time. Darwin proposed that three factors are responsible for changes in the plant and animal world:

1. natural selection, the selection of random differences in color, shape, or other physical attributes in a species that help the plant or animal survive;

2. the direct influence of the environment causing weaker individuals to die out because of their

24

inability to adapt to harsh climate or poor food availability;

3. the effects of use or disuse of certain distinctive traits such as a long neck that allows for better food gathering or coloration that disguises the animal in its surroundings.[2] The proper coloration or an effective food-gathering technique might enable one group of animals to survive while another group dies off.

Darwin's Published Works

Darwin did not invent the ideas of evolution and natural selection by himself. Many scientists experimented with their own evolution theories at the same time. The English scientists William Charles Wells in 1813 and Patrick Matthew in 1831 both formulated theories of natural selection. Darwin did not know of their work, however. Alfred Russel Wallace, another English scientist, revealed in 1858 that he was ready to propose the same theory of evolution as Darwin's theory. Darwin and Wallace both published brief versions of evolution theories in 1858. Then in 1859, Darwin hurried to finish the final version of his book *On the Origin of Species by Means of Natural Selection.*[3]

In this book, Darwin did not mention human beings as part of the evolutionary process of natural selection. Darwin explored the idea of human evolution

Charles Darwin developed a theory that attributed the physical differences between animal species to a process called natural selection.

in his next major work, *The Descent of Man*, published in 1871. Darwin was familiar with the views of religious people who thought only God could be responsible for creating life. He realized his book created much controversy and conflict between religion and science. Nonetheless, he argued that animals adapted and changed because of interaction with their environment. He did not believe that these adaptations necessarily had anything to do with a single act of creation by God.

Much debate focused on *The Descent of Man*. Society's reaction to Darwin reminded historians of the great Italian scientist Galileo. He proved scientifically in 1632 that Earth revolved around the Sun. The Roman Catholic Church taught that Earth was the center of the universe. All planets and stars revolved around Earth, and God placed mankind on Earth to enjoy the treasures of Creation. The Catholic Church banished Galileo when he opposed their views. Likewise, ministers and older scientists ridiculed Darwin for his ideas. Later, however, the Church of England reversed itself and accepted Darwin's views. When he died, Darwin was lionized, or elevated to a place of great importance, and buried at Westminster Abbey in London.

Darwin himself did not attempt to disprove the existence of God in his scientific observations of the natural world. But he knew that his research would be considered blasphemous (showing irreverence toward God) and heretical (advocating an opinion contrary to church teaching). At the end of *The Descent of Man*, Darwin wrote, "the main conclusion arrived at in this work, namely that man is descended from some lowly-organized [sic] form, will, I regret to think, be highly distasteful to many."[4]

Sympathetic with church leaders, Darwin wrote letters to his American friend Asa Gray. Gray was a great botanist and a leading member of an evangelical Protestant Church. In one letter to Gray, Darwin said that he failed to find evidence of a good creator God when he studied a particular species of wasp. The wasp tortures its victims before eating them. Darwin wrote, "there seems to me too much misery in the world. I cannot persuade myself that . . . God would have designedly created the [wasp] . . . or that a cat should play with mice."[5]

Asa Gray defended Darwin's theories, and he came to believe that there is no conflict between evolution and creationism. Though he believed in God, Gray's research of the varieties of plants in Asia and North America showed that the plants were variations of a single species. Gray's work confirmed Darwin's theory of natural selection. Darwin did not accept Gray's views about God, but the two scientists remained lifelong friends. Darwin himself did not see his evolution theory as conflicting with religion. But Darwin wrote that he was deeply confused about the suffering that seems to happen in nature. In another letter to his friend Asa Gray, he wrote, "I feel most deeply that the whole subject is too profound for the human intellect. A dog might as well speculate on the mind of Newton. Let each man hope and believe what he can."[6]

The Social Gospel Movement

A new movement within Christianity was beginning to make use of Darwin's ideas. Some church leaders were able to accept Darwin's theory right away; evolution with its emphasis on change seemed consistent with the new Social Gospel Movement—"an 'onward and upward' brand of theology."[7] The Social Gospel Movement sought to apply Christian principles to a variety of social problems caused by the modern world. The movement's leaders tried to tackle problems like industrialization, urban crowding, crime, and the dehumanization of factory workers by teaching religion and dignity to the working class.

Evolution became a political and religious issue only after the famous trial of John T. Scopes in Tennessee in 1925. Before 1925, evolution was taught as a new scientific theory that showed how plants and animals adapted to their surroundings. During the nineteenth century, evolution was a regular component of biology teaching in America's high schools. In the twentieth century, America rapidly expanded. Many immigrant groups from Europe, including many Jews and Catholics, increased the population of the public schools. The Social Gospel Movement attempted to spread its beliefs to the new Americans.

The Fundamentalists

Protestant rural America did not like the new immigration and argued against the Social Gospel

John T. Scopes (left), shown here with his father, was the first to bring the issue of evolution to the courts. Only after Scopes's case did evolution become a political and religious issue.

Movement. Evangelicals, Christians who emphasize spreading their faith through talking to others, published a pamphlet series called *The Fundamentals* between 1909 and 1912.[8] These pamphlets called for a literal reading of Genesis and the Bible as a response to modern changes. Because of the pamphlets they produced, the Christians came to be known as Fundamentalists. They traveled through midwestern and southern states, trying to restrict the teaching of evolution. Between 1920 and 1926, eight southern states made it illegal to teach evolution. The Fundamentalists used a simple and highly effective message that made sense to many people: God directly inspired the writers of the Bible. People must interpret the Bible literally and believe it infallibly, or beyond doubt. Fundamentalists taught that the Creation story in Genesis, the first book of the Bible, is literally true in every word. God created man and woman specially to rule over the animals and over the earth, according to the Bible. Fundamentalists believed that evolution promoted false, immoral, and anti-American ideas that were contrary to those presented in the Bible.

Many States Pass Laws Against Darwin's Theory

Following the Monkey Trial of John T. Scopes, many states like Mississippi, Arkansas, Oklahoma, Florida,

Texas, Louisiana, and Tennessee passed laws against teaching Darwin. In all, twenty states held similar laws.[9] Some church leaders wanted a constitutional amendment forbidding the teaching of evolution.

The antievolution law in Arkansas, originally passed in 1928, confused many teachers. According to the Arkansas Statutes Annual of 1929, section 80-1627 prohibited the "Doctrine of Ascent or Descent of Man From Lower Order of Animals." The law made it unlawful for any teacher

> in any university, college, normal, public school, or other institution of the state, which is supported in whole or in part from public funds derived by state and local taxation, to teach the theory or doctrine that mankind ascended or descended from a lower order of animals. . . . Any teacher or other instructor or text-book commissioner who is found guilty of violation of this act . . . shall be guilty of a misdemeanor and upon conviction shall be fined not exceeding five hundred dollars and upon conviction shall vacate the position thus held in any educational institution above mentioned.[10]

Susan Epperson would fight her battle based on this law. It appeared to restrict teachers at all levels from kindergarten through college from talking about Darwin's theory of evolution.

3

On the Road to the Supreme Court

The Arkansas Education Association (AEA), a professional group of teachers and educators associated with the National Education Association, knew about the 1928 law. The teachers did not like the fact that the law restricted biology teachers in Arkansas and limited what students could learn. Teachers could be fired if they even casually mentioned evolution in class. Forrest Rozzell was the executive secretary of the AEA. He had known about the law for many years. He wanted to challenge it, so he formed a committee of teachers determined to take a stand against it. In their public statement sent to newspapers, the teachers said the law was "an impediment to quality public education in Arkansas."[1]

Some teachers feared the law was a sleeping giant. It had never been enforced or tested. They thought the giant was better off ignored and unawakened. They feared the law would be called on to prosecute and to dismiss teachers who chose to teach Darwin's theory of evolution. But was the giant really as big as teachers feared? Did people in Arkansas still feel so strongly against evolution that students should not know about the widely accepted theory of how life changed over time?

Avoiding the Mistakes of the *Scopes* Trial

Forrest Rozzell wanted to avoid repeating the frenzied and emotional carnival atmosphere that surrounded the *Scopes* trial. Rozzell knew that publicity would certainly follow this case. If Rozzell and the AEA were to test the law, everyone in the state would suffer the consequences. The national media might portray Arkansas as a backward southern state still clinging to old-fashioned beliefs. It was the 1960s, an era of progressive change. The United States was involved in a race with the Soviet Union to put the first man on the moon. Science education received new emphasis across the country. Many states tried to upgrade teaching in science and math. Rozzell wanted to avoid publicizing Arkansas as antiscience.

Rozzell plotted his strategy to challenge the Arkansas law for several months. First, Nathan Schoenfeld, a Garland County State Representative, tried to repeal the law by sponsoring a resolution in January 1965. The bill failed to pass through committee and was never called for a vote.[2] The *Arkansas Gazette* praised Schoenfeld for trying to bring Arkansas into the modern era.

Several Groups Join Rozzell

Public interest and knowledge of the Arkansas law grew. Suddenly, opinions started appearing in the newspapers. People wrote letters to the two Little Rock newspapers, the *Gazette* and the *Democrat*, expressing different points of view. Several groups as well as individuals wrote statements expressing their views about Rozzell's planned challenge of the antievolution law. The American Association of University Women (AAUW) joined Rozzell in expressing opposition to the law. The Central Baptist Association countered the AEA's statement about the law being "an impediment to quality public education." It said that evolution should remain out of the Arkansas schools. Many other editorials and letters to the editor followed in the newspapers. Some opposed and some expressed support for Rozzell. The Arkansas State Association of Missionary Baptist Churches passed a resolution challenging the state to enforce the law. The Arkansas Teachers' Association and the Arkansas Negro Teachers' Association created resolutions supporting the AEA and its desire to repeal the 1928 law.[3]

Even John T. Scopes got involved in the discussion. (By that time he had retired from teaching and was living in Louisiana.) "The issue is not whether the theory of evolution is true," said Scopes. "That wasn't the issue in my trial—but the issue of whether or not a man can say what he wants, teach what he wants, think what he wants."[4]

Rozzell thought that legal action would be more effective than a vote by the people. The issue was far too emotional and mixed up with religion to be objectively decided by a popular vote. The voting public might not be able to give a resolution a fair hearing. Rozzell knew that the freedom of teachers to teach and students to learn was the issue, not religion.

Rozzell Consults an Attorney

Rozzell's next step was to consult with Eugene R. Warren, attorney for the AEA. Warren agreed with Rozzell that the antievolution law contradicted both the state and federal constitutions.[5] Most important, Rozzell hoped Warren could help him file a lawsuit.

Crisis in Little Rock

People still remembered the Little Rock integration crisis of 1957. State militia troops were called to keep African-American students out of Central High School. When the Supreme Court handed down its decision in *Brown* v. *Board of Education,* blacks and whites could go to Arkansas schools together for the first time. However, Governor Orval Faubus refused to honor the law that allowed blacks and whites to attend the same schools together. He used the Arkansas National Guard to prevent it. President Dwight D. Eisenhower met with Governor Faubus to force him to withdraw his troops. Then Eisenhower ordered the same Arkansas National Guard troops to protect nine African-American students from angry crowds surrounding Central High.[6] The schools were finally integrated. Rozzell feared repeating the violence, bad national publicity, and interference with education that followed the integration crisis.

Still in office in 1965, Governor Faubus was one of many people opposed to Rozzell's effort to repeal the antievolution law. Governor Faubus supported the law as "a safeguard to keep way-out teachers in line."[7]

Little Rock, Arkansas's Central High School, where Susan Epperson taught, was known for its 1957 integration crisis.

Attorney Warren felt that the law was vague and indefinite. What did it mean that it was illegal "to teach Darwin's theory?"[8] How would a teacher violate this law? Would a teacher be in violation for having an encyclopedia or dictionary in the classroom that defined Darwin's theory? Most such standard reference works include a mention of Darwin. Could a teacher just say that Darwin's theory exists, without endorsing it? Too much was uncertain about this law.

Strategies Continue

Rozzell and Warren continued to plot their strategy. Warren decided that the Arkansas law should be tried by the United States Supreme Court. It involved constitutional issues of free speech and the establishment of religion. But getting to the Supreme Court was not the easiest thing to do. First, several lower courts would need to hear the case. Then, the Supreme Court would have to decide that the case was important enough to review. The Supreme Court selects only a few of the thousands of cases it receives each year.

In the United States, there are two separate court systems—state and federal. Each state has its own system made up of city courts, county courts (known as chancery courts in Arkansas), state district courts, state appellate courts, and the state Supreme Court. The state system deals with violations of the state's criminal laws, traffic violations, divorce, murder, contract disputes, and other civil laws.

The federal system handles matters of national interest such as income-tax evasion, federal drug-law violations, and constitutional issues such as those of freedom of speech or religion. The United States Supreme Court is the highest legal authority, and it can review decisions made by either the state or federal courts. If a question about the Constitution is raised in a case, it will be better served in the federal system. However, Warren was afraid that the Little Rock school board would not want to make a constitutional issue out of the case. The school board saw the argument as having to do with local control over the curriculum. Warren thought the best path to the United Sates Supreme Court would be through the Arkansas state system, not the federal system.

The Search for a Plaintiff

Rozzell and Warren began searching for a suitable plaintiff, the person who would be named in the lawsuit, to test the Arkansas antievolution law. Rozzell consulted his close friend Virginia Minor. She was a kindergarten teacher at Little Rock Central High School. (Kindergarten classes in the Little Rock schools were located at the high schools.) Minor was also president of the Little Rock chapter of the American Association of University Women (AAUW). It was one of the groups that had publicly expressed support for repealing the law.

Susan Epperson taught biology at Central High School, the same school where Virginia Minor taught kindergarten. Epperson knew about the AAUW. She had discussed the AAUW's stand on the antievolution law with Minor. When Rozzell asked Minor to help him find a plaintiff for the lawsuit, Minor immediately recommended Susan Epperson.

Minor introduced Epperson to Rozzell and Warren.

Rozzell discovered that he knew Epperson's parents. He had attended the College of the Ozarks, where Epperson's father, Dr. Thomas L. Smith, taught biology.[9]

Epperson knew of the law and the restrictions it placed on biology teachers in Arkansas. For the 1965–66 school year, the textbook selected for the tenth grade by the Little Rock school district was *Modern Biology* by James Otto and Albert Towle. The Otto and Towle book had been the most popular and widely used biology textbook for many years. First published in the 1920s, the book was cleaned of references to Darwin's theory of evolution after the 1926 edition. Following the *Scopes* trial, publishers feared mentioning evolution in their textbooks. They thought that if they did, nobody would purchase the textbooks for school use.

Arkansas Textbooks in Violation of Law

Evolution was reintroduced in the 1965 edition. Several statements in the book brought the new edition into direct violation of the Arkansas law. For example, the book said:

> In 1871, the English biologist Charles Darwin published his famous book entitled *The Descent of Man*. Darwin proposed that the same forces operating to bring about changes in plants and animals could also affect man and his development.[10]

These images by famous artist Michaelangelo evoke images of God and a "higher power"—not Darwin's theory of evolution.

The Otto and Towle textbook stated that many anthropologists believed humans evolved along separate lines from the primates, or apes. However, the two species may have had a common ancestor.[11]

How did a textbook mentioning evolution, which broke the state law, get selected by the school board? The textbook selection committee was made up of teachers and headed by the Assistant Superintendent for Instruction. The committee was probably unaware of the antievolution law. Talk about the law had largely been restricted to more rural areas of Arkansas. Now, the Schoenfeld resolution, letters to the editor, and statements by the AAUW appearing in newspapers in Little Rock were prominent. More people began to take an interest in the law.

In 1965, almost every biology text discussed evolution. A school board would be hard-pressed to find a biology text that did not at least mention Darwin and his theory. It was not until after the Institute for Creation Research was founded in 1970 that alternative biology textbooks on "intelligent design theory" became available.[12] This theory meant that some intelligent creative power (like God) must have designed all the varieties of plant and animal life found on Earth. The theory used modern scientific language for the same view of Creation expressed in Genesis.

Epperson had two choices. She could obey the law and deny a professional responsibility to teach current biology, or she could break the law by using the Otto and Towle textbook. If she did this, she faced possible prosecution and dismissal.[13] The situation seemed hypocritical to Epperson. There was no way to carry out her job. She had hoped that the old law would be repealed.

In November of 1965, Epperson, Minor, Rozzell, and Warren met in Minor's kindergarten classroom. Rozzell wanted to know if Epperson would accept the lead role and help the AEA to challenge the old law. Sitting on tiny chairs around a pint-sized desk, they discussed matters of great importance. The legal issues in the AEA lawsuit, the Constitution of the United States, the 1928 law, the possible bad publicity and what it meant for Epperson and her family were all discussed. Epperson agreed to become the plaintiff in the suit. She sympathized with the difficult situation for Arkansas biology teachers. She thought the lawsuit would help all students and science teachers in the state.

In her written statement to the press, Epperson said:

> I do not try to teach my students what to think. I try to teach them how to think, how to make sound judgments. . . . It is my responsibility to expose my students to and encourage them to seek after as much of the accumulated scientific knowledge and theories as possible.
> When Mr. Rozzell asked me to become the plaintiff

in this test suit I agreed to do so because of my concept of my responsibilities both as a teacher of biology and as an American citizen.[14]

Epperson also said that "if you've studied some science . . . you understand that evolution is a very unifying principle. . . . To leave it out, . . . is really short-changing your students."[15] Epperson thought that a teacher is someone who should set an example and be an example to students. Being named in this lawsuit was simply a way of living out her philosophy.

Instead of just having the name of a professional organization, the "AEA suit," the lawsuit would now be the Epperson challenge to the state's law. Epperson's role in the lawsuit went way beyond merely supplying her name. She had a commitment to teaching and a strong desire to promote constitutional freedoms for Arkansas education. Her participation in preparing for the trial supplied the lawyers with information essential to writing their briefs. (Briefs are written legal arguments presented to the judge before the trial begins.) Rozzell, Warren, and Epperson formed a resourceful, supportive, and energized team ready to fight the law.

Getting the Case Heard

Warren had decided that the best route to the United States Supreme Court would be through the Arkansas court system. There were two chancery courts in which

Susan Epperson accepted the lead role in helping the Arkansas Education Association challenge the antievolution law. She agreed to become the plaintiff in a lawsuit.

the case could be filed. However, people who filed lawsuits did not get to choose; cases assigned to chancery courts took odd or even numbers, going to either Judge Williams or Judge Reed. Warren wanted the case heard by Judge Murray O. Reed. He was a legal scholar who would see the constitutional issues in the *Epperson* case. Reed would not get distracted by the religious fervor, emotion, and publicity that plagued the *Scopes* trial. Reed kept tight control over his courtroom and would not allow another "Monkey Trial."[16]

On December 6, 1965, Warren was ready to file the *Epperson* suit. He wrote two different lawsuits to file— the *Epperson* suit and another unimportant "place-holder" lawsuit. If Judge Reed had the next opening as the numbers were drawn, Warren would file the *Epperson* suit and get started. If Judge Williams had the next opening, Warren would file the place-holder suit with him, and get the *Epperson* suit to Reed. Warren's strategy ensured that Judge Reed would hear the *Epperson* case no matter what happened.

The next day, readers of the *Arkansas Gazette* saw the headline "Teacher at Central High School Challenges Constitutionality of Evolution Law." The newspaper assisted Epperson's cause with an editorial praising her efforts on behalf of teachers and championing intellectual freedom.

Soon, however, people were writing angry letters expressing their disagreement with Epperson: "As the United States is mostly Christians, this is an affront to Christians," said one. "I cannot stand people who deny and go against God. Go on, teach evolution and may God have mercy on your soul. . . ."[17]

Constitutional Rights of Teachers and Students

To Warren and Epperson, the lawsuit had nothing to do with religion, science, or the validity of Darwin's theory. The issue centered upon the constitutional rights of teachers and students. Warren thought *Epperson* v. *Arkansas* stood the greatest chance of success if it focused on freedom of speech and the Establishment of Religion Clause of the First Amendment. Epperson's constitutional rights of free speech and freedom from "official" religion were being violated by Arkansas. Warren's main argument would be that the Arkansas antievolution law conflicted with the Due Process Clause of the Fourteenth Amendment. The Arkansas law was "vague and indefinite."[18]

Warren and Epperson wanted academic freedom preserved. Warren thought that the First Amendment guarantee of free speech also extended to teaching and learning. When Arkansas restricted its public school curriculum and excluded evolutionary biology, it restricted free speech and learning.

The Case Goes to Chancery Court

Warren filed in the Pulaski County Chancery Court on December 6, 1965, on the grounds that the Arkansas antievolution law violated state and federal constitutions. The *Epperson* lawsuit against the Arkansas antievolution law was scheduled for April 1, 1966— April Fool's Day, as noted by several journalists. Judge Reed made no secret of his contempt for the old law. He allowed the case only one day for hearing rather than the two weeks requested by the state. Arkansas attorney general Bruce Bennett defended the law for the state of Arkansas. Bennett was a conservative Democratic politician—someone who believed that everything was fine just the way it was. He was famous for helping Governor Orval Faubus to fight court-ordered desegregation. Many newspapers pointed out superficial similarities between Epperson's lawsuit and the trial of John T. Scopes in Tennessee. Journalists compared Bennett to William Jennings Bryan—a comparison Bennett himself invited. They also compared Warren with Clarence Darrow. Warren wanted nothing of this comparison. He sought to avoid a high-profile trial.

Bennett had his eyes on the upcoming Democratic

primary election for governor. Governor Faubus had announced his decision not to seek reelection. Bennett wanted to raise public awareness of his abilities by staging a flamboyant defense of the law. If he could model himself after William Jennings Bryan, the skillful orator who prosecuted John T. Scopes, Arkansas citizens might remember him and vote for him for governor. Bennett wished to recreate the atmosphere of the *Scopes* trial. He planned to use many emotional arguments and scientific witnesses against evolution. It would be a war of modern science against old-time religion. This was not helpful to Rozzell, Warren, and Epperson's case.

Epperson Compared With Scopes

Epperson and Scopes were both twenty-four-year-old teachers at the time of their trials. Beyond having plaintiffs of the same age, however, the *Epperson* and *Scopes* trials had nothing in common. Spectacle-seekers and journalists hoped the *Epperson* trial would showcase flashy cross-examinations and wild theories, but it did not. People came to Judge Reed's court to experience history in the making. Most, however, would be disappointed by the trial itself.

A crowd of over one hundred people crammed into the courtroom on April 1, 1966. An overflow audience

Judge Murray Reed presided over the chancery court in Pulaski County, Arkansas, that heard the *Epperson* case.

was pushed out into the hallway. For extra precaution, three bailiffs were on hand to perform any needed service. This was two more than usual. (A bailiff is an armed and uniformed member of city or county law enforcement who escorts witnesses in and out of court and helps put down disturbances to the legal process.) Judge Reed wisely prohibited radio, television, and photography from the trial.

Warren introduced the antievolution law. The first witness was Hubert H. Blanchard, Jr. He had added his name to the *Epperson* lawsuit because he thought his two sons in Little Rock high schools were denied freedom to learn. Blanchard was assistant executive secretary of the AEA. He had complained to the Little Rock schools that his two children were not receiving instruction in accepted theories of science.[19] As a taxpayer and officer of the AEA, Blanchard wanted his sons to receive the best education possible. His children should not be restricted to just one point of view in biology class.

Epperson's Testimony

The next witness was Susan Epperson. Her testimony was directly aimed at supporting the reasoning of the suit. She had this to say:

> I brought this lawsuit because I have a textbook which
> includes the theory about the origin or the descent or
> the ascent of man from a lower form of animals. This
> seemed to be a widely accepted theory and I feel it is
> my responsibility to acquaint my students with it.[20]

Warren asked Epperson a few more questions, then Bennett jumped in to attack. Bennett asked Epperson how she planned to teach Darwin's theory of evolution. He also asked about her beliefs concerning Darwin's theory. Warren stood up to object. Bennett and Warren were good friends outside the courtroom. Warren, however, was not going to let Bennett stray from the real issue. Each time Warren objected to Bennett's line of questioning, Judge Reed allowed the objection. Warren objected to Bennett's questioning a total of sixty-three times during the trial. This strategy successfully undermined Bennett's attempt to inject religion into the trial.[21]

Next, Bennett tried to challenge Epperson's knowledge of philosophy, history, and science. Bennett, however, was poorly prepared and not well educated about science himself. He made serious mistakes in reasoning and pronunciation. His errors caused the courtroom audience to laugh several times. "This is a serious matter," Judge Reed warned the audience following the laughter. "The only question here is a constitutional question of law and it is a serious one."[22]

Judge Reed cautioned that he would clear the courtroom if laughter continued.

Bennett's planned-for dramatic defense of the Arkansas law, modeled after William Jennings Bryan's defense of the Tennessee law, was a huge failure. Many things had changed in the forty years since the *Scopes* trial. In 1925, both the Tennessee law and the court's assumptions about teaching evolution favored the state. Evolution was a new idea then, and most people did not like it. Back then, Bryan simply asserted Tennessee's legal authority to regulate teachers. He fought off Darrow's efforts to prove the law unconstitutional. In *Epperson* v. *Arkansas,* Judge Reed's view of evolution and the Constitution favored Epperson, not the state. Warren's strategy was simply to assert Epperson's constitutional right to teach evolution. The strategic positions for the arguments for and against evolution in the *Epperson* case were exactly the reverse of those in the *Scopes* case. In the *Scopes* case, most people disliked evolution. In *Epperson* v. *Arkansas,* most people accepted evolution. Warren could use that in his favor.[23]

There was one defense Bennett used that was not objected to by Warren. It was based upon the testimony of school superintendents and school board members. Bennett asked if they had received complaints about the antievolution law having a negative effect on schools. The superintendents said they had not.

No Courtroom Drama

Those who hoped to see a great courtroom drama left disappointed. The *Epperson* trial did not relive history with a new Bryan and a new Darrow. Too many things had changed since then.

Two months later Judge Reed issued his opinion:

> This Court is of the opinion that a chapter in a biology book, adopted by the school administrative authorities, stating that a specific theory has been advanced by an individual that man ascended or descended from a lower form of animal life, does not constitute such a hazard to the safety, health and morals of the community that the constitutional freedoms may justifiably be suppressed by the state.[24]

Arkansas Law is Judged Unconstitutional

Judge Reed determined that the Arkansas law was unconstitutional. Susan Epperson could now teach evolution to her biology class. Unfortunately, this would last for only one year.

The effect of the court's ruling was not so much to legalize Darwin's theory as to allow educators to teach and students to learn without interference from a local school board. However, during the year that teaching

Attorney General Bruce Bennett attempted to challenge Susan Epperson's knowledge of biology after Judge Reed refused to allow questions about religion or creationism during the trial.

about evolution was allowed, the status of Darwin's theory in science classrooms did not change. The ruling simply made the teaching of evolution legal in the urban districts where it had already been taught for many years. In the more rural parts of Arkansas, schools ignored the ruling and continued to forbid the teaching of Darwin's theory. The case would need to be appealed to a higher court.

Ruling Appealed to a Higher Court

Attorney General Bennett appealed Judge Reed's ruling to the Arkansas Supreme Court. Bennett and Warren saw the Arkansas Supreme Court as just a stopping point on the way to the United States Supreme Court. They both had very different reasons for wanting to get to the Supreme Court, however. The Arkansas Supreme Court apparently understood this. Its opinion was very brief, and no reasoning was given to back up its finding. No previous decisions were discussed. On June 5, 1967, the Arkansas Supreme Court gave a two-sentence ruling, saying that the state law

> is a valid exercise of the state's power to specify the curriculum in its public schools. . . . The court expresses no opinion on the question whether the Act prohibits any explanation of the theory of evolution or merely prohibits teaching that the theory is true.[25]

Eugene Warren was the attorney for the Arkansas Education Association, the group that initiated the legal challenge to the antievolution law.

The State Supreme Court supported the antievolution law as constitutional. After being legal for just over one year, Epperson would once again be violating a law if she taught evolution. Warren's argument had been that the law was vague and uncertain. The Arkansas Supreme Court said nothing about that. Susan Epperson was again faced with a dilemma. Again, there was much uncertainty about the standing of Arkansas teachers and the teaching of evolution.

For the most part, biology teachers at Central High School in Little Rock were already teaching Darwin's theory of evolution, and had been for many years. They did not know they were in violation of a law—it was never enforced. Science teachers kept on teaching evolution in Little Rock. Teachers in small towns, however, never even thought of mentioning Darwin. His theory went against the religion of most students there. The antievolution law was on the books, but it meant nothing. Students living in small towns would never learn about evolution, while their city counterparts *would* get an education in scientific principles. Susan Epperson found this unacceptable. The case was on its way to the Supreme Court.

4

Susan Epperson Goes to the Supreme Court

Susan Epperson readied herself to go to trial before the United States Supreme Court in 1968. Meanwhile, America struggled with some long-standing conflicts. The Vietnam War was the biggest of them. Americans argued with each other over whether to continue fighting against communism in Vietnam. The space race with the Soviet Union was in full swing. Americans were anxious to see who could put a man on the moon first. Struggles over civil rights, free speech, and drug experimentation were also a part of the late 1960s.

In Chicago, hundreds of Vietnam War protesters fought to have their complaints heard at the

Democratic National Convention. Chicago mayor Richard Daley used National Guard troops to calm the disturbances. Young leaders like President John F. Kennedy and Senator Robert Kennedy had been gunned down by assassins. Senator Ted Kennedy waited in the wings at the Democratic National Convention. He worried about whether he could carry on his family legacy and lead the country through troubled times.[1]

Susan Epperson anxiously awaited her appeal to the Supreme Court.

The Supreme Court Hears the Case

On October 16, 1968, the trial was set to begin. The Air Force had assigned Epperson's husband to the Pentagon. This is the center of military administration in Washington, D.C. She was living in Maryland at the time of the trial and was no longer a teacher of biology. During the trial, Justice Black commented that Epperson was no longer teaching in Arkansas. As such, she was not under any threat of prosecution from the antievolution law.

Why should the Supreme Court hear the case if Epperson did not teach biology any more? The fact that Epperson had left Arkansas did not mean that other science teachers could not benefit from the freedom to discuss Darwin's theory. Mississippi still had an antievolution law that would be affected by this case. If Epperson were victorious, hundreds of teachers and students in those two states would have the freedom to discuss Darwin.

Bruce Bennett, the Arkansas attorney general from the two previous trials, had not won reelection in 1966. Joe Purcell had won the election to become Arkansas's attorney general. Don Langston, assistant attorney general, also came to Washington for the Supreme Court trial to oppose Epperson; he would present the oral arguments.[2] Eugene Warren, the AEA attorney who had won the first lawsuit, was assisted by Bruce T. Bullion, a Little Rock attorney.

Langston and Epperson, adversaries in the trial about to begin, chatted easily. They had known each other in college at Clarksville. Now, they were surprised at where their different paths had taken them.

Arguments Begin

Eugene Warren started the argument as he had before, saying that the case involved the constitutionality of the Arkansas antievolution law. Susan Epperson and Hubert Blanchard, father of two students in Arkansas, were challenging the constitutionality of the so-called "Monkey Bill."[3] Epperson and Blanchard contended

Bruce Bennett (left) lost the election to regain his seat as attorney general of Arkansas in 1966. His loss was due, in large part, to the publicity of the *Epperson* case. Joe Purcell (right) won the election to become attorney general of Arkansas.

that the law violated the First Amendment freedoms of speech and learning, and it raised the question of freedom of religion. According to the First Amendment, "Congress shall make no law respecting an establishment of religion, or prohibiting the free exercise thereof." By prohibiting the teaching of evolution, Arkansas promoted one religious viewpoint (Christianity) over others.

Purpose of Antievolution Law Questioned

Warren explained how the antievolution law failed to serve a purpose. He referred to its vague nature under the Due Process Clause of the Fourteenth Amendment. According to that clause, no state can "deprive any person of life, liberty, or property, without due process of law." This means that states cannot pass laws that prevent citizens from constitutional protections and equal access to the legal system. Warren said:

> From the time this act was enacted or adopted, teachers in Arkansas were genuinely confused and concerned, uncertain as to whether or not the language . . . forbids the teacher to discuss the matter . . . or whether the actual meaning of the act was that the teacher could not teach that the theory was true.[4]

Warren argued that Epperson did not want to be in deliberate violation of the state's antievolution law. However, she was furnished with a biology book by the school district that contained a chapter on evolution. He added that no textbook existed that did not have some reference to the theory of the evolution of man.

Establishment of Religion Argument Presented

Justice William J. Brennan, Jr., questioned Warren about whether he was taking "the first position" under the First Amendment. The First Amendment says that "Congress shall make no law respecting an

Bruce Bullion was the Little Rock attorney who assisted Eugene Warren in the preparation and writing of legal briefs for *Epperson* v. *Arkansas*.

establishment of religion, or prohibiting the free exercise thereof; or abridging the freedom of speech, or of the press, or the right of the people peaceably to assemble, and to petition the Government for a redress of grievances." So Justice Brennan was asking whether Warren's argument was that the Arkansas law attempted to establish a religion. Warren answered yes.

66

Justice Brennan also questioned Warren about three other cases or precedents related to Epperson's suit. They were *Bartels* v. *Iowa* (1923), *Meyer* v. *Nebraska* (1923), and *Ginzburg* v. *United States* (1966). In the *Bartels* case, the plaintiff was a teacher convicted of teaching students below the eighth grade to read in German. This went

Eugene Warren, who represented Susan Epperson at the Supreme Court level of her trial, questioned the constitutionality of the antievolution law in Arkansas.

against an Iowa law that required instruction in English. The Supreme Court struck down the law under the Due Process Clause of the Fourteenth Amendment. In *Meyer v. Nebraska*, the Supreme Court struck down a Nebraska law prohibiting teaching of modern languages other than English to children before the eighth grade. Meyer taught in a private school. He used a German Bible as a reading text because most of his students were from German immigrant families. The Court said the Nebraska law, like the Iowa one, violated the Due Process Clause of the Fourteenth Amendment. In *Ginzburg* v. *United States*, the Court upheld a publisher's conviction for selling obscene materials. Several Justices did dissent, however. They held that the finding represented a restriction on free speech. This case showed that the kinds of "speech" protected by the First Amendment were not limited to antigovernment or overly politicized statements. Even classroom teaching could be considered speech protected by the First Amendment.

Should Age of Students Be a Factor?

The reason Justice Brennan asked Warren about the *Bartels* and *Meyer* cases is that they referred to state laws that drew lines of distinction depending on the age of students in school. The laws restricted teaching in the earlier grades. Justice Brennan wanted to know if this related to the Arkansas law. While Brennan tried to probe the question of the students' age, Warren used the opportunity to draw attention to who ought to set school policy. Warren answered that "The position of the public schools, even in the elementary grades, is not a matter for ballot, but a matter for the proper education officers."[5] Warren pointed this out because Epperson was restricted by an Arkansas law initiated by some Christian citizens, not by educators.

Referring to the decision of the Arkansas Supreme Court, Warren asserted that the court did not decide whether the act forbids the discussion of the theory or forbids teaching that the theory is true.[6] Warren believed that this avoided the core of the issue. The law's vagueness made enforcement impossible. Should a teacher be constrained by an ill-defined law where conviction results in dismissal from her job? The law also required a $500 fine. This was a lot of money for a teacher in 1928. At that time, the average public school teacher earned $1,433 per year. In 1968, at the time of the *Epperson* trial, the average public school teacher earned $7,129 per year.[7]

During Epperson's trial, Justice Black asked if anyone had ever been prosecuted. Warren said that he knew of no one. Teachers, however, may have felt the constant threat of prosecution. Some prosecutions had been started, but none was ever finished. The law had to have some potential for enforcement in order to be taken seriously. Warren said:

> I can't say there was any danger or not. There was a lot of uncertainty and a lot of fright. I think the act was used mostly [as a] bogeyman. In a number of districts in Arkansas, the subject of biology is not even taught. In other districts in Arkansas, because the biology books do have chapters [on Darwin], when the teacher reaches that chapter, the teacher simply skips it . . . the teacher announces that the reading of this chapter is illegal. I think the children probably run and read it and get more from that chapter than any other.[8]

Law's Restriction of Textbook Use Questioned

Wanting to drive home his point about the law's vagueness, Warren then rose to one of the few emotional peaks in the trial. He reminded the court that the antievolution law forbids use of a textbook containing Darwin's theory. He questioned the meaning of the word "use." Is a teacher liable for prosecution if she refers to a book that mentions Darwin? As Warren inferred, a teacher's reference to a book is use of that book. *Webster's International Dictionary, Webster's Collegiate Dictionary,* and all encyclopedias and general reference works of the time included some explanation of Darwin's theory. Would anyone recommend restricting students' use of these resources? Warren argued that "if the act has that sort of meaning, then that means that every school has got to rid its library of all these books. This is just plain ridiculous. That is book burning at its worst."[9]

The Justices questioned Warren's reasoning on this point. They wondered if the Arkansas law actually reaches so broadly as to include everything Warren said it did. One Justice said the law only makes it unlawful for a teacher to adopt for regular classroom use a Darwin book as a textbook. This did not necessarily include reference works. The text of the law itself does not reach such a specific level.

Warren answered that the question of a book's being a textbook or a reference work did not clear up the vagueness of the law. He pointed out that school districts in Arkansas had adopted a dictionary as a textbook and supplied it to classrooms. He further noted that

> a teacher couldn't refer a student to the dictionary for fear that that student inadvertently might turn to the page that had the explanation of evolution on it, and then the teacher is subject to dismissal from her position.[10]

Warren Concludes His Argument

Warren concluded his argument before the Supreme Court by saying that the law is "clearly vague, clearly unconstitutional." Epperson's First Amendment free-speech rights were violated because she could not teach a certain subject in the public schools. Moreover, the First Amendment Establishment of Religion Clause was violated. The state of Arkansas appeared to be preferring one religion, Christianity, over others. The Fourteenth Amendment Due Process Clause was also violated by the Arkansas law. The state's law took the place of Arkansas's citizens' constitutional rights.

Biblical Authority Not on Trial

None of these points had anything to do with science versus religion. Warren and Epperson did not have to put biblical authority on trial. They did not wish to criticize any Christian who believed in the Genesis story of Creation. Nor did they want to prove scientifically that Darwin's theory was the best or only explanation for how life changes. Epperson and Warren merely wanted to establish constitutionally guaranteed freedoms for students in Arkansas and Mississippi. Now they waited to hear what counter argument Don Langston and Joe Purcell would offer. What kind of defense of the Arkansas antievolution law would they mount?

5

Arkansas Responds to Epperson's Lawsuit

Don Langston, assistant attorney general for Arkansas, started to argue his case. He did not specifically use creationist views to defend the Arkansas law. Those views would not be allowed in the Supreme Court. Because they were specifically religious, their inclusion would be in violation of the Constitution. But the creationist movement is related to the original reason Arkansas enacted its antievolution law in 1928. Christians called Fundamentalists did not like the fact that scientists were teaching that human beings evolved from a lower primate form and that humans were possibly related to other apelike species. Let us turn away from the Supreme Court trial for a moment and trace the background of the creationist movement.

The Creationist Movement

The argument between creationism and evolution concerns the heritage of the human species. It also involves the theory of how all of life first began on Earth. Creationists believe that God created Earth and all its life-forms. Many scientists in the fields of biology and geology believe life began when certain inorganic chemicals came into contact with each other. This process formed the first organic molecules. Creationists dislike this "molecules to man" concept. These first living single-celled creatures, so the theory goes, evolved into more complex organisms. Eventually they evolved into primates and human beings.

Christians strongly disagree with the molecules to man theory. This was an extension of Darwin's original theory. Fundamentalists thought it was an attempt to eliminate God from having anything to do with the story of Creation.

Langston Begins His Defense

Chief Justice Earl Warren (not to be confused with attorney Eugene Warren) asked Langston to begin his defense. The first thing Langston said was that Susan

Joe Purcell appeared at the Supreme Court trial but he did not present any of the oral arguments in the case.

Epperson had initiated her lawsuit in 1965. This was prior to the term of office of present attorney general, Joe Purcell. Langston said the previous attorney general, Bruce Bennett, had defended the law in the state courts. Bennett had not won reelection, so he was not in the Supreme Court to continue his defense.

Chief Justice Warren asked why Langston was giving this statement at the beginning of his defense, and suggesting that "your administration doesn't like the statute."[1] Langston answered that he was not prepared to say that. Before Langston began his arguments, Justice Abe Fortas said that "it might not be too late [for Langston to say that the state does not like the law]."[2] Whatever Langston wanted to say, he certainly did not attempt a passionate Bryan-like defense. According to *The New York Times*, "Mr. Langston made it clear that the attorney general's office was defending it only because the law required it to. His apparent lack of enthusiasm for the case had the Justices and courtroom visitors in laughter on several occasions."[3]

Langston said that when a lawsuit is initiated "seeking to have any state statute [law] declared unconstitutional," the attorney general's office must be involved. Langston said he interpreted this to mean that the Arkansas laws are constitutional and must be defended as such. This included the 1928 antievolution law. In case the Justices thought that nobody in Arkansas took the law seriously, Langston noted that in the Chancery Court, Judge Reed filed "what I would call a rather lengthy opinion for a trial court in Arkansas."[4] Langston said that the Supreme Court could rely on the reasoning of the Chancery Court for its decision. He added, however, that the Arkansas Supreme Court merely issued a per curiam opinion without giving their reasoning. A per curiam decision means that a higher court is overruling a lower court.

Langston explained that he did not know why the Arkansas Supreme Court did not file a written opinion backed up with reasoning. He then attempted to clear up the confusion about what would constitute a violation of the law. Justice William J. Brennan, Jr., asked, "How would a teacher know if she broke the law?" Langston replied that "to make a student aware of [Darwin's] theory, not to teach whether it was true or untrue, but just to teach that there was such a theory would be grounds for prosecution."[5] To the Justices, this seemed like a remarkable restriction against the freedom of teaching and learning. The Justices questioned Langston on this point. The assistant attorney general of Arkansas continued to say that to "teach" meant to make a student aware of Darwin's theory. Simply mentioning Darwin would be a violation of the law. The teacher did not have to say the theory was valid or not valid.

What Constitutes "Teaching"?

According to Langston's interpretation, if Epperson told her students, "'Here is Darwin's theory that man ascended or descended from a lower form of being,' then I think she would be under this statute liable for prosecution."[6] But the Justices had difficulty with Langston's interpretation of the Arkansas Supreme Court's two-sentence ruling because of its brevity. The second sentence of the Arkansas Supreme Court's decision said that "it expresses no opinion" about whether the act prohibits "explanation" of the theory of evolution or merely forbids "teaching that the theory is true."[7] Langston attempted damage control by saying that "the lower courts of Arkansas would hold that [second] sentence irrelevant . . . although the Supreme Court of Arkansas did not."

Was the Antievolution Law Unconstitutional?

The Supreme Court wanted to get to the heart of the matter. The question was whether the Arkansas law violated the First and Fourteenth Amendments. The Justices stated that the constitutionality must be decided on the basis of the interpretation of the law in a state court. But where was the interpretation in this case? Langston answered that it was in the first sentence of their ruling. The law "is a valid exercise of the state's power to specify curriculum in the public schools."[8]

One issue yet to be addressed was the level of education meant to be controlled by the law. Did the law refer to primary grades, high schools, colleges and universities, or some combination of all of them? The law mentioned no specific educational level.

Was the Law Age Specific?

The lack of a specific educational level to which the law applied opened up the problem of impressionable minds. Younger students might be especially vulnerable to defective ideas. Langston said that the student's age made no difference. The Arkansas law meant to exclude teaching evolution to anybody at any educational level. This denies the teacher any right to teach Darwin even in college, well beyond the impressionable years. The Court attempted to press Langston on this point. It said, "you are defending [the law] on the ground that it is constitutional and you deny the teacher any right to teach this even in college?"

Langston did not answer this question immediately. He said he could defend the law against the charge that it was "vague and uncertain." In the *Scopes* trial, the court held that the Tennessee law was valid. It met the requirements that it was not vague and uncertain. "We think our statute is even better worded than theirs [Tennessee's]. So therefore, in the light of that decision and our statute, we think that it meets the constitutional test of due process."[9]

State's Right to Control Curriculum Defended

Langston's most passionate defense of the law came under the theme of the state's freedom to set its own curriculum. This theme touched a nerve with many people in Arkansas. Many believed that the federal government had been too quick to issue regulations affecting people in many states without consulting them. Some of Langston's arguments implied that disorder and chaos would rule if the state did not attempt strict control over curriculum. Perhaps this was a reference to the disorder and fighting that broke out in Little Rock following integration in 1957.

Against the charge that the law violated the Establishment of Religion Clause of the First Amendment, Langston said the Arkansas law had religious neutrality. The law "could keep the discussion of the Darwin Case versus the Bible story out of the teachings in the public schools and keep them outside that forum, in private forums."[10] Thus Arkansas schools could continue the orderly management of their classrooms. The whole creationism versus evolution debate could rage on outside the walls of the government-funded public schools.

The Supreme Court was concerned that the law ruled out a major branch of knowledge. But was it because a particular group of Christians found Darwin's theory unacceptable? Should public school students be allowed to consider even controversial ideas? Should the schools have the power to throw out any branch of science if they found its content objectionable or offensive?

Chief Justice Earl Warren asked if Langston would defend a law prohibiting the teaching of a theory that some races are inferior to others. Langston answered that that should be prohibited. "What about making it illegal to teach geometry?" Chief Justice Warren also asked, "What about forbidding teaching that the Earth is round?"

What Boundaries Should the Law Have?

Langston responded that "there is going to have to be a line drawn here somewhere. But where exactly does a state draw the line?" "That is our problem, too," said Warren. Langston said he realized that the trend of the

Supreme Court is to strike down laws that infringe against personal liberties. But, he said,

> Here we have reasonably done it [ruled out one kind of knowledge]. As to the teaching of geometry . . . we may not reasonably do it. But here we think we have not been unreasonable and that the judgment of the Supreme Court of Arkansas should be affirmed.[11]

Langston said he felt strongly that the courts should refrain from meddling in the schools' business. As much as possible, local school boards should decide what curriculum is adopted.

Justice Potter Stewart answered back that the law in question does not have to do with the specific subject to be taught—history, mathematics, or foreign language. This law pertains to a certain theory of Creation. He added,

> [The law] simply forbids the teaching of the Darwin theory, doesn't it? Isn't [forbidding teaching that some races are inferior to others] rather similar to the [Arkansas] statute? What if Arkansas would forbid the theory that the world is round?[12]

Langston continued to argue for the reasonableness of the Arkansas law. He did not say that it was a valid restriction of free speech. Returning to the subject of the grade level, one Justice asked Langston if he saw any connection between the Arkansas law and *Meyer* v. *Nebraska* (1923). Langston answered that the teaching of German in the early grades in school would be unreasonable. Restricting teachers from teaching Darwin's theory could be considered reasonable. This would be true if the intent was to stay away from the religious aspects of the theory.

Wait a minute, thought the Justices. Did not Langston just say that prohibiting the teaching of evolution was meant to prevent conflict with the biblical story of Creation and "the literal reading of the Book of Genesis"? If the purpose of the law is to prefer one religion over another, it runs right into the question of the First Amendment.

Did the Law Serve a Religious Purpose?

"If [the law] does not serve a religious purpose, what purpose does it serve?" asked the Justices. In other words, if the Creation theory could be taught but evolution could not, the law was indeed promoting one religion over another.

Toward the end of the questioning, Justice Thurgood Marshall directed this question to Langston: Since the Arkansas Supreme Court had disposed of the lower court's opinion in two sentences, would he object to the United States Supreme Court disposing of the law in one sentence? Langston did not answer Marshall's question directly. He only repeated that the law is a "neutrality act." He meant that Arkansas tried to create neutrality toward religion by having an antievolution law. However, this statement was not supported by any evidence or logic.

Arkansas Law Biased Against One Theory Among Many

The Justices concluded their questioning with an observation. There are many theories of the origin of man. Arkansas eliminated only one segment—Darwin's theory of evolution. Chief Justice Warren said that "there is no general prohibition . . . against discussing how a man came into being, and there is no general prohibition so that theories including the Bible, the literal reading of Genesis, could be discussed in the schools."[13] Langston agreed that Warren's statement was correct. He did not respond to the implied violation of the First Amendment Establishment of Religion Clause. In other words, Warren ended the oral arguments by getting Langston to admit that the Arkansas law directly violated the First Amendment. It preferred the Christian view of Creation over any other view, including Darwin's theory of evolution. The oral arguments concluded. There was no solid counter-argument against the charge of violating the First Amendment.

6

Epperson v. Arkansas Reaches a Conclusion

During the *Epperson* case, Chief Justice Earl Warren presided over the Court. According to legal scholar Bernard Schwartz, the Warren Court era of 1953–1969 was one of the "two great creative periods in American public law."[1] The other was the Court of Chief Justice John Marshall of 1801–1836. America changed rapidly during the 1950s and 1960s. The country grew quickly following the end of World War II. It entered the Vietnam War and the Civil Rights era. These were two periods of great conflict between activist individuals and more conservative institutions of society. The role of Chief Justice Warren's court was to keep up with rapid social change. Some of these social changes are reflected in *Epperson* v. *Arkansas*. This case reflects new understandings of religion. It also broadens what kinds of speech are protected by the First Amendment. Finally, it limits government control of school curriculum.

Chief Justice Earl Warren

Chief Justice Warren's background reflected the changes in American society happening during the 1950s and 1960s. Warren was born in 1891 and raised in Los Angeles (just a small town then). It was a place that still showed traces of the vanished frontier. Cowboys, ranchers, and saloons were familiar to Warren as a boy. The town, and the state of California, quickly changed. It became urban, economically powerful, multiracial, interested in individual liberties, and plagued by social justice issues.

Like the state of California, Warren had changed in many ways. Before his appointment to the Supreme Court, he was governor of California. At that time, Warren "had a simple belief in the things we now laugh at: motherhood, marriage, family, flag, and the like," according to Justice Potter Stewart.[2] Warren supported the forced evacuation of Japanese-Americans from California, Oregon, and Washington into internment camps after the surprise bombing of Pearl Harbor, Hawaii, in 1941 during World War II.

As the Chief Justice, however, he began the "Warren revolution." It lasted until his retirement in 1969. Warren was a great leader. He was less concerned with legal scholarship and precision than with social justice and political change. The Supreme Court under Warren encouraged the shift away from protecting property rights to the protection of personal rights and freedoms.[3] In case after case, Warren showed that he wanted to respect the integrity of individual freedoms. He fought to expand the rights guaranteed to individuals.

Other Important Warren Cases

During the *Brown* v. *Board of Education* integration case in 1954, Warren strongly supported racial equality for blacks and whites. Warren fought hard to get a unanimous vote to overturn the old "separate but equal" doctrine of *Plessy* v. *Ferguson.* He established the "one man, one vote" districts in *Reynolds* v. *Sims* (1964). He also was behind the prohibition of prayers in public schools in *Engel* v. *Vitale* (1962). He helped require that a suspect be informed of his or her rights, be provided with a free attorney, and be given the right to remain silent in *Miranda* v. *Arizona* (1966). He also led the Warren Commission. This was the government committee that investigated the assassination of President John F. Kennedy in 1963.

Warren had been appointed by President Eisenhower in 1953. Three years earlier when Eisenhower battled for the Republican party nomination, then-governor of California Earl Warren gave his support to Eisenhower. Warren said he wanted to be remembered if any Supreme Court seats ever became available. After Chief Justice Vinson died in his sleep of a heart attack, Warren was nominated. Eisenhower appointed Warren while the Senate was in recess. In this way, Warren did not have to wait to be confirmed before beginning his duties.[4]

Eisenhower had further opportunities to influence the direction of the court. He wanted to staff the Supreme Court with Justices supportive of his political views. A year after his appointment of Warren, Justice Jackson died. To replace him, Eisenhower selected New York attorney John Marshall Harlan. Eisenhower also named New Jersey Supreme Court Judge William J. Brennan, Jr., following the retirement of Justice Minton in 1956. Brennan became the first Justice to serve on the Court who was born in the twentieth century. Then, Justice Reed retired, and Eisenhower named federal judge Charles Whittaker to succeed him. Eisenhower named his fifth Justice when Justice Burton retired. He chose federal judge Potter Stewart.

Chief Justice Earl Warren presided over the Supreme Court in the *Epperson* v. *Arkansas* case.

A Court With Moderate Views

All five new Justices had in common their moderate views. The Warren Court would take a great interest in civil rights, individual liberties, and protection of constitutional rights. Many decisions made by the Warren Court in the 1950s and 1960s showed protection of individual liberties.

The Warren Court broadened the interpretation of the personal rights guaranteed by the Constitution. This was especially true in the area of freedom of expression. Two members of the Warren Court, Justices Black and Douglas, argued for an extreme view of freedom of speech whenever the First Amendment applied to a case being discussed. Black and Douglas believed that the language of the First Amendment was unqualified: "Congress shall make no law . . . abridging the freedom of speech." They viewed this as saying with absolute clarity that no law, under any circumstance, can be passed against free speech, even speech that is obscene or threatening to others. The Warren Court did not adopt this absolute view. It did, however, emphasize the protection of freedom of speech. This is important to *Epperson* v. *Arkansas*. After all, Eugene Warren, the attorney for the Arkansas Education Association, used the argument that the Arkansas antievolution law was unconstitutional because it violated the First Amendment.

Precedents for the *Epperson* Decision

In the ruling of the *Epperson* case, the Warren Court had to consider important previous cases related to freedom of speech and school control. These things would be compared with Epperson's circumstances. Supreme Court Justices frequently referred to four precedents that turned out to be very important to *Epperson* v. *Arkansas*, *Meyer* v. *Nebraska* (1923), *Everson* v. *Board of Education* (1947), *McCollum* v. *Board of Education* (1948), and *Keyishian* v. *Board of Regents* (1967).

Everson v. *Board of Education*

In *Everson* v. *Board of Education* in 1947, the Court upheld a New Jersey state law that provided free bus service to schoolchildren, including those attending religious schools. To New Jersey resident and plaintiff Arch Everson, this law violated the Establishment of Religion Clause of the First Amendment. Everson believed taxpayer money should not be used to support any religious institution. However, the Supreme Court upheld the law. It held that the state must not be the enemy of religious institutions. The case showed how the religion clauses of the First Amendment are applied to the states by the Fourteenth Amendment. That amendment says that states cannot pass laws that override constitutional freedoms. *Everson* v. *Board of Education* set the standard by which religion clauses in the Constitution are interpreted. The meaning of the *Everson* opinion is that neither the state nor the federal government can set up a religion. "Neither a state nor the Federal Government can pass laws which aid one religion, aid all religions, or prefer one religion over another."[5] The Court used this precedent in the *Epperson* case to show that Arkansas might be trying to support one particular religious view over another.

McCollum v. Board of Education

In *McCollum* v. *Board of Education* (1948), the Court ruled that the state of Illinois could not release students from class to attend religious instruction in public school buildings. This would involve using tax-supported property for religious purposes. Unlike *Everson*, *McCollum* showed that the state could become overactive in support of one religion over another.[6]

Keyishian v. Board of Regents

In *Keyishian* v. *Board of Regents* (1967), the Court declared unconstitutional a New York law designed to prevent the employment of subversive teachers. The New

York Board of Regents had prepared a list of "subversive groups." The Communist party was among the groups listed. The Court held that the New York law was unconstitutional because of vagueness. A teacher could not know whether statements about an abstract doctrine were illegal or whether only speech intended to cause action was grounds for dismissal. The Court rejected the state's power to make employment conditional upon the surrendering of constitutional rights.[7]

In these cases preceding *Epperson* v. *Arkansas,* the Court was interested in protecting academic freedom. It also wanted to avoid interference by the state or federal government into school control. The Supreme Court showed in the *Meyer* and *Keyishian* cases that students and teachers do not surrender their constitutional rights when they enter a school building. In the *Everson* and *McCollum* cases, the Court demonstrated that preferring or hindering any one religion in the public school is unconstitutional. These cases showed that the Supreme Court was interested in protecting and broadening constitutional freedoms and rights. This point was especially important to Epperson's defense.

Justices Discuss the *Epperson* Case

After hearing the oral arguments in the *Epperson* case, the Supreme Court spent approximately one month deliberating. On Friday, October 18, the Supreme Court convened to discuss Epperson's case. The question to be resolved was not whether to strike down the Arkansas antievolution law. Don Langston as much as admitted the law was unconstitutional during the arguments. This was proven true especially at the conclusion when he had no response to the challenge that Arkansas law violated the Establishment of Religion Clause of the First Amendment. The real question deliberated by the Court was: On what legal grounds should the law be struck down? The Justices tossed around three main arguments about how the Arkansas law violated the Constitution: (1) its vagueness, (2) its implied establishment of religion, and (3) its restriction of freedom of speech.

On What Grounds Should the Law Be Struck Down?

Chief Justice Earl Warren, Justice Hugo Black, and Justice William Douglas agreed with Epperson's attorney, Eugene Warren. "The Act [was] too vague to stand."[8] Justice Douglas argued that he did not think establishment of religion was really presented in the oral arguments by AEA attorney Warren. Warren did not present any evidence that the Little Rock public schools were trying to promote Christianity exclusively over other religions.

Justice Potter Stewart said he thought that the law restricted teachers' freedom of speech. Justices Harlan, Brennan, White, Fortas, and Marshall believed the Arkansas law violated the First Amendment's Establishment of Religion Clause.

After all the discussion ended, it became obvious that a unanimous decision would be appropriate. Every Justice thought the Arkansas law was unconstitutional

The 1967–68 Supreme Court that decided *Epperson* v. *Arkansas* is shown. Seated from left to right: John M. Harlan, Hugo L. Black, Earl Warren William O. Douglas, and William J. Brennan, Jr. Standing from left to right: Abe Fortas, Potter Stewart, Byron R. White, and Thurgood Marshall.

in some way. They each agreed that the law should be removed from the Arkansas legal system. They differed slightly in their reasoning, however. Justice Abe Fortas volunteered to write the Court's opinion.

Justice Abe Fortas

Fortas was a fifteen-year-old Jewish boy growing up in Memphis, Tennessee, at the time of the *Scopes* trial. He had vivid memories of the trial. He admired John Scopes for standing up against an unjust law. Fortas saw Susan Epperson as a modern-day John Scopes. He applauded her efforts at striking down the out-of-date Arkansas law. Fortas thought the Tennessee antievolution law had been a disgrace to the state. Epperson was removing that blemish from Arkansas's reputation.

The Court Issues a Unanimous Opinion

Fortas issued the Court's unanimous opinion on November 12, 1968, by noting the parallel between Scopes and Epperson:

> This appeal challenges the constitutionality of the "anti-evolution" statute which the state of Arkansas adopted in 1928 to prohibit the teaching in its public schools and universities of the theory that man evolved from other species of life. The statute was a product of the upsurge of "fundamentalist" religious fervor of the twenties. The Arkansas statute was an adaptation of

the famous Tennessee "Monkey Law" which that state adopted in 1925.[9]

Fortas wrote that the Arkansas statute went against the First Amendment. It was also in violation of the Fourteenth Amendment. The First Amendment guarantees freedom of religion. The Fourteenth Amendment makes the guarantee binding on the states. The Arkansas law went against the First Amendment's Freedom of Speech and Establishment of Religion clauses. Fortas condemned the law as needing to be struck down. It violated the Constitution in many ways through its narrow focus:

> The overriding fact is that the Arkansas law selects from the body of knowledge a particular segment which it proscribes for the sole reason that it is deemed to conflict with a particular religious doctrine; that is, with a particular interpretation of the book of Genesis by a particular religious group.[10]

Fortas wrote that Epperson faced a "literal dilemma" in September 1965 when she was presented with a new biology textbook containing a chapter on Darwin's theory of evolution. She was "supposed to use the new textbook for classroom instruction and presumably to teach the statutorily condemned chapter, but to do so would be a criminal offense and subject her to dismissal."[11]

Fortas said that

> Government in our democracy . . . must be neutral in
> matters of religious theory, doctrine and practice. It
> may not be hostile to any religion or to the advocacy
> of non-religion; and it may not aid, foster or promote
> one religion or religious theory against another.[12]

Fortas did agree that the state and local school board
authorities do have power to shape curriculum. The
absolute execution of their power, however, is limited in
areas that conflict with constitutional values:

> By and large, public education in our nation is com-
> mitted to the control of state and local authorities.
> Courts do not and cannot intervene in the resolution
> of conflicts which arise in the daily operation of school
> systems. . . . On the other hand, the vigilant protec-
> tion of constitutional freedoms is nowhere more vital
> than in the community of American schools.[13]

Other Cases Related to *Epperson*

Regarding other precedents related to the *Epperson* case,
Fortas pointed to the 1923 decision *Meyer* v. *Nebraska*.
There the Supreme Court overruled a Nebraska law
making it a crime to teach in any language other than
English. Fortas said the Court recognized the purpose
of the Nebraska law. It acknowledged the state's power
to prescribe curriculum for the schools. The Court
ruled, however, that these considerations were not

adequate to support the restrictions on the freedoms of teachers and students.

Concurring Opinion

Justice Hugo L. Black concurred in the Court's unanimous decision. However, he expressed the view that it was doubtful whether the case presented a controversy over which the Court should rule. He did not think the Court had a reason to take up the issue of academic freedom. Assuming the case was capable of being ruled upon, either the law should be struck down as too vague to enforce or the case should be sent back to the Arkansas Supreme Court for clarification of its opinion. Justice Black wrote that "although the statute was passed by the voters of Arkansas in 1928, we are informed that there has never been one single attempt by the state to enforce it."[14] Black saw no evidence that the Blanchard children had not been instructed in Darwin's theory. He said that Epperson had given up her teaching post and moved to a distant city. She effectively escaped any possible punishment by the state of Arkansas. Black disagreed that the federal government should be thrust into state school curriculum issues. The state of Arkansas's weak interest in this case did not prompt it to keep the Court informed. For example, there may have been aspects of the case that might have justified dismissal of the lawsuit as moot (lacking legal merit for debate) or lacking genuine qualities of a controversy.

Justice John Marshall Harlan concurred in the decision. He thought, however, that the Arkansas Supreme Court's reluctance to give reasoning in their decision was a studied effort to avoid coming to grips with this old law. The Arkansas Supreme Court attempted to "pass the buck" to the United States Supreme Court.[15] Justice Harlan thought constitutional claims had been properly raised; thus resolution by the Supreme Court could not be avoided. But he disapproved of the Court's extended discussion of the issues of vagueness and freedom of speech. It had originally concluded that it was unnecessary to decide such issues. Justice Harlan felt this discussion obscured the meaning of the decision itself. It was made primarily on the violation of the Establishment of Religion Clause of the First Amendment. The Court struck down the law because Arkansas advocated a government-sponsored, official religion, not because the law violated freedom of speech.

Justice Potter Stewart also concurred with the decision. He expressed the view that the law was so vague as to be invalid under the Fourteenth Amendment.

Justice Stewart thought that the state is free to choose curriculum for its schools, but not so free as

> to make it a criminal offense for a public school teacher to so much as mention the very existence of an entire system of respected human thought. That kind of criminal law, I would think, would clearly impinge upon the guarantees of free communication contained in the First Amendment, and made applicable to the States by the Fourteenth.[16]

Because of the vagueness of the law, Justice Stewart said that Arkansas teachers were never sure when or if they were in violation.

Differing Reactions to the Decision

AEA attorney Eugene Warren later said he did not think the Court's decision would be based on such firm deliberation over the establishment of religion issue. In an interview, Warren said, "it came as a complete surprise to me, the Court's decision based on the Establishment Clause."[17]

Forrest Rozzell and the AEA were overjoyed with the Supreme Court's decision. Because of Rozzell, Susan Epperson, and Eugene Warren, the Court had affirmed the freedom of teachers and students to inquire, to study, and to evaluate ideas. Epperson said that the Court's decision would allow Arkansas science teachers to "teach the full subject of biology with an open mind and clear conscience." Epperson said she thought "all biology teachers of the state, even if they did not break the law, always had a cloud over their heads" when the time came to discuss evolution.[18]

Many people thought that *Epperson v. Arkansas* put an end to all the controversy about evolution and creationism. This was the Court's first ruling on this issue. It had established a precedent to which other court cases would refer in handling similar disputes. Following the *Epperson* decision, an article titled "The End of the Monkey War" appeared in *Scientific American*.[19] John T. Scopes himself uttered prophetic words after the *Epperson* decision. Living in retirement in Shreveport, Louisiana, Scopes said that just because the *Epperson* case was over did not mean that there was no work left to do. Scopes also said, "The fight will go on with other actors and other plays. You don't protect any of your individual liberties by lying down and going to sleep."[20]

Life After Epperson

This truth became clear in the decades following *Epperson v. Arkansas*. Creationists tried new, more effective tactics to influence school curriculums in many states.

In Arkansas, schoolteachers said that they were

happy the antievolution law had been struck down. However, many teachers had been ignoring the law for years anyway. Eugene Warren said "We are very happy that the Supreme Court has finally had an opportunity to strike down a law which was archaic and created ridicule toward Arkansas."[21]

Many school officials and church leaders attempted to downplay the significance of the *Epperson* v. *Arkansas* decision. It was, however, a victory for academic freedom and free speech for teachers and students. Even some ministers thought the Court's decision to overturn the law was justified. Reverend M. L. Moser, Jr., was the pastor of the Central Baptist Church in Little Rock. Moser said he thought "teachers teach that evolution is a fact and that only those who are ignoramuses reject the theory of evolution." But Moser also said he thought creationists "should be allowed to teach their views [whenever] the theory of evolution is presented."[22]

Arkansas State Education Commissioner Arch W. Ford was not surprised. He had expected the Court to make the decision overturning the law. He noted that the textbooks currently in use in Arkansas contained Darwin's theory. Local school districts select textbooks, not the state, but the Arkansas schools used the same textbooks as schools in other states. He added that "No problem of adjustment is involved, because the books contained the theory, anyway, and it is said that the teachers teach it despite what the law has said."[23]

The dust eventually settled in the case of *Epperson* v. *Arkansas*. Forrest Rozzell went back to his job with the AEA. Eugene Warren returned to his regular attorney business. Susan Epperson continued working in the Washington, D.C., area until her husband's career in the Air Force took them elsewhere. Students in Arkansas could enjoy the freedom to learn biology and evolution without the threat or fear of losing their teacher for it. Creationism would always be an alternative, religious theory about the beginning of life on Earth—and most students in Arkansas would probably be familiar with creationism through their religious beliefs. The Supreme Court had made it clear: Arkansas could not have an official religion supported by its public schools. Students were free to believe anything they chose, but the state could not exercise its power of promoting one particular religion over another.

7

Where Do We Go
After Epperson?

Following the *Epperson* decision in 1969, people thought the creationism versus evolution arguments that began in the 1920s were over. Just prior to *Epperson* v. *Arkansas* in 1967, Tennessee lawmakers had repealed the Butler Act. This law was the law or statute used to prosecute John T. Scopes. Arkansas's anti-evolution law had been struck down because of Susan Epperson's suit.

California Creationists
Confront Science Education

In California, however, an intense new assault on science education began in 1969. Creationists learned that if they could demonstrate to school boards that scientific creationism had evidence to support it and, therefore, credibility, schools would get new textbooks more accepting of creationism. This new strategy would mean that schoolchildren would learn to associate creationism with science, not necessarily with religion.[1]

California's state board of education revised the state's guidelines for science curriculum about every five years. An advisory panel of scientists recommended changes to the curriculum to the state board of education. Usually, the advisory panel went with mainstream scientific research and progress. For example, the advisory panel had said that evolution is a "major organizing principle of the life sciences."[2]

One member of the advisory panel agreed with creationists and wanted more active support for their views. Vernon Grose was an aerospace engineer who belonged to a conservative Christian church. He suggested an amendment to the science guidelines. With the change, they would describe evolution as a less than certain theory. Creationism would be described as real science, no less valid than evolution. The science advisory panel rejected most of Grose's suggestions. The California Board of Education appreciated Grose's revisions, however, and tried to help his efforts. Many of the board members were also

Christians. They had been appointed by then-governor Ronald Reagan. During the three-year discussion about Grose's proposed revision to the science guidelines, nineteen Nobel Prize winners asked the board not to include creationism in the science curriculum. The Nobel scientists argued that creationism, as a theology or philosophy, was not appropriate for science courses.

Creationists fought back by attacking the theory of evolution itself. They claimed that natural selection means the origin of the world itself was a matter of accident. This signified a major shift in the strategy of creationists. The antievolutionists of the 1920s argued that evolution theory was too restrictive and denied human free will. Now creationists were saying that evolution was too chaotic and allowed too much freedom and randomness.[3] Creationists believe a creator-God must have been behind a deliberate, planned act of creation.

The California Board of Education endorsed Vernon Grose's revisions. It fought with its own textbook commission, however, for several years about what to add to the science books. Eventually, the board reached a compromise in saying that evolution is a theory, not a fact. In 1972, it agreed to remove absolute statements about evolution from science books. Such statements would be replaced by conditional statements. Creationism as a philosophy about the origin of life could be taught in *social* science courses. It should not be taught in biology courses.[4] Still, this was a significant victory for creationism. It opened a loophole for its reentry into the public schools.

California governor Ronald Reagan left office in 1975. His successor, Governor Edmund "Jerry" Brown, Jr., appointed members to the board of education who eventually dropped the idea of teaching creationism in social science classes. The board retained Grose's conditional statements made about evolution, however. Evolution could be taught as science in biology classes, but not as an absolute fact. It would be described as a theory, something not completely accepted or proven.

Creationism and Evolution on Equal Ground

The new strategy embraced by creationists was that if public schools taught evolution, they should also teach creationism in equivalent proportions. This "equal time" philosophy rang up some impressive victories during the 1970s. The first such proposed law came in Tennessee in 1973. This was only six years after Tennessee had repealed its antievolution law. The proposed new law required "equal attention and emphasis to other ideas of creation, including those contained in the Bible." This would balance evolution

The creationist movement received an unexpected endorsement from
Ronald Reagan in 1980.

with biblical creationism. A Tennessee court ruled that the law's reference to a particular religious perspective violated the First Amendment of the Constitution.[5]

Although the Tennessee law did not pass, the creationist movement achieved success in influencing policies that did not require legal action. These include the decisions of local school boards about textbook selection. The creationist movement enjoyed increasing acceptance and influence. It scored victories in textbook selections in Texas, Georgia, Alabama, and local school boards in Ohio, West Virginia, Arkansas, Florida, and Missouri.

Ronald Reagan Endorses Creationism

The creationist cause received an unexpected endorsement in September 1980 by presidential candidate Ronald Reagan. He told a meeting of Christian leaders that:

> Evolution is a theory, it is a scientific theory only, and it has in recent years been challenged in the world of science and is not yet believed in the scientific community to be as infallible as it once was believed. But if it was going to be taught in the schools, then I think also the Biblical theory of Creation, which is not a theory but the Biblical story of Creation, should also be taught.[6]

Reagan never publicly mentioned creationism again,

and his administration did not have any written policy about it. However, this was a significant endorsement coming from a politician who would be the president of the United States for the next eight years. Several politicians had attempted to use the teaching of evolution as an example of America's moral decline. If America returned to an earlier, more Bible-centered culture, the reasoning went, our educational standards and test scores would rise.

Segraves v. California

Scientific creationism was in the spotlight in 1981. The legal case of *Segraves* v. *California* came to trial when the Creation Science Research Center (CSRC) sued the state of California. The center sought to prevent thirteen-year-old Kasey Segraves, son of one of the CSRC directors, from being taught the theory of evolution. Judge Irving Perluss rejected nearly all of the plaintiff's arguments. He did, however, reaffirm the California policy that evolution should not be taught as an absolute fact. Also in 1981, Arkansas lawmakers passed the first of the modern equal-time laws. It required that scientific creationism—not biblical creationism—be taught whenever evolution is taught. Even though the Supreme Court had ruled against teaching biblical creationism in *Epperson* v. *Arkansas,*

111

the state now had a law allowing for scientific creationism.[7] Biblical creationism relies on Genesis and other scriptural texts. Scientific creationism uses geology and scientific facts to prove the theory of creation.

Edwards v. Aguillard

In 1982, lawmakers in Louisiana passed a law requiring that any public school teaching evolution must grant equal time to the theories of Creation Science. Don Aguillard, a Lafayette biology teacher, filed a lawsuit against the state's governor, Edwin Edwards. The suit became known as *Edwards* v. *Aguillard.*

The Supreme Court listened to arguments on December 10, 1986. Jay Topkis of the American Civil Liberties Union argued that the Louisiana law lacked scientific merit and merely endorsed one religion. The creationists' attorney, Wendell Bird, argued that the Louisiana law was supported by abundant scientific research and facts. He wanted the Court to order a full trial on the law. In this way, factual evidence could be presented, including theories, models, evidence, hypotheses, books, tracts, films, videotapes, and witnesses. The creationist institutes had now been operating for about fifteen years. They had produced volumes of information supporting their views.

On June 19, 1987, the Supreme Court issued its decision. Seven of the nine Justices concurred that Louisiana's equal-time law was unconstitutional. It violated the First Amendment. The decision said the Louisiana law intended

> to advance the religious viewpoint that a supernatural being created humankind. The term "creation-science" was defined as embracing this particular religious doctrine by those responsible for the passage of the Creationism Act. . . . The legislative history documents that the Act's primary purpose was to change the science curriculum of public schools in order to provide persuasive advantage to a particular religious doctrine that rejects the factual basis of evolution entirely.[8]

Justice William J. Brennan, Jr., said that the Louisiana law did not intend to increase the comprehensive nature of all science education. It merely wanted to advance the views of one particular group. Brennan thought that the law did not protect academic freedom; it only wanted to discredit evolution by countering it with creationism every time the facts were presented.

Antievolution Pressure Builds

Meanwhile, other antievolution activists have increased their pressure on the public schools to include their views in teaching science. In 1994 in Tangipahoa

Parish, Louisiana, "the school board adopted a policy requiring science teachers to read a disclaimer whenever evolution is presented in textbooks, workbooks, pamphlets, or other written materials." The disclaimer reads that the teaching of evolution is "not intended to influence or dissuade the biblical version of Creation or any other concept."[9]

In 1995 in Alabama, the state board of education voted to place a disclaimer in all biology textbooks used in public schools. The disclaimer says that evolution is a "controversial theory" accepted by "some scientists" and adds that "no one was present when life first appeared on Earth. Therefore, any statement about life's origins should be considered as theory, not fact."[10] Alabama governor Fob James endorsed the statement. He also used his discretionary funds to purchase more than nine hundred copies of an antievolution book, *Darwin on Trial,* by Philip Johnson, and send them to all the biology teachers in the state.[11]

In 1996 in Cobb County, Georgia,

> a science textbook committee made up of administrators, teachers, and parents asked the publisher of a fourth grade science textbook to remove the final chapter, titled "The Birth of Earth. . . ." It did not include Creation as a possible theory for the origin of the universe. The publisher . . . agreed to delete the offending chapter.[12]

Lawmakers in Georgia, Ohio, and Tennessee have recently tried to pass antievolution bills in their states, but none has succeeded. A Democratic state senator in Tennessee authored a bill that would have allowed districts to fire teachers who present evolution as fact rather than theory. If passed, this law would have been similar to the Arkansas law struck down by the Supreme Court in *Epperson v. Arkansas.*

There have been two Supreme Court rulings saying that creationism in the public schools violates the First Amendment. Nonetheless, the battle continues.

Susan Epperson's lawsuit did not put an end to creationist attempts to change school curriculum.

Supporters of creationism have succeeded in persuading millions of Americans that scientific evidence supports a biblical or religious interpretation of the beginning of life. They have done this despite the fact that scientific methods make *no* statements pertaining to religion. Public opinion polls report that 40 percent of adults surveyed think creationism is scientifically as valid as evolution.[13]

As long as people fear that America is facing the decline of education, the family, society, and government, there will always be people who will spread the message that evolution is part of the problem. These people say that if we return to a more religious and conservative morality in the public schools, America might return to its former glory. But this reasoning supposes that the past is better than the present or future and that public schools can endorse one particular religious view. While the first point is open to interpretation, the second is unconstitutional.

Epperson v. *Arkansas* stands as a lesson that the United States will not tolerate unchanging or one-sided versions of the truth in its schools. Academic freedom allows all teachers and students to question and to learn the full range of knowledge in all subjects. This includes the freedom to decide which theory of the beginning of humankind is best suited to our own personal beliefs.

Questions for Discussion

1. Read the First Amendment of the Constitution of the United States. To what extent does freedom of speech extend to the classroom? How much authority do teachers have to suppress certain viewpoints and opinions that may be objectionable?

2. Why would it be wrong for the government to prefer one religion over another? Think of some examples of what would happen if the government required that you practice a particular religion.

3. The text of the Fourteenth Amendment states that "no State shall abridge the privileges or immunities of citizens of the United States; nor shall any State deprive any person of life, liberty, or property, without due process of law." How was the *Epperson* case offensive to this amendment?

4. At what point in history did courts start reading the Fourteenth Amendment to include not only property rights but also personal liberties? When did people begin to get more vehement in their defense of their constitutional rights as American citizens?

Chapter Notes

Chapter 1. Susan Epperson's Dilemma

1. *The Holy Bible*, Revised Standard Version, Genesis 1:14-26 (New York: Thomas Nelson & Sons, 1952), p. 1.

2. David Hill, "Counter Evolutionary," *Teacher*, November/December 1996, p. 24.

3. Watchtower Bible and Tract Society of New York, *Life—How Did It Get Here?: By Evolution or by Creation?* (New York: Watchtower Society, 1985), pp. 8–9.

4. Richard Current, T. Harry Williams, and Frank Freidel, *American History: A Survey Since 1865* (New York: Knopf, 1979), vol. 2, p. 621.

5. Garry Wills, *Under God: Religion and American Politics* (New York: Simon & Schuster, 1990), p. 128.

6. Hugh Ross, *Creation and Time: A Biblical and Scientific Perspective on the Creation-Date Controversy* (Colorado Springs: NavPress, 1994), p. 34.

7. Hill, p. 24.

8. *Epperson* v. *Arkansas* (Supreme Court of the United States, Transcript of Decision, No. 7, 1968), p. 8.

9. Susanna McBee and John Neary, "Evolution Revolution in Arkansas," *Life*, November 22, 1968, p. 89.

10. Ibid.

11. Ibid.

12. *Epperson* v. *Arkansas* (Decision), p. 2.

13. Ibid.

14. Ibid.

15. Fred P. Graham, "Children, Says the Court, Should Be Seen and Heard," *The New York Times*, November 17, 1968, section 5, p. 4.

16. Wills, p. 124.

Chapter 2. Two Theories Behind the Conflict

1. Charles Darwin, "Natural Selection," in *A World of Ideas*, ed. Lee A. Jacobus (Boston: Bedford Books, 1994), p. 401.

2. Ibid.

3. Ibid., p. 402.

4. Charles Darwin, *The Descent of Man, and Selection in Relation to Sex* (Princeton, N.J.: Princeton University Press, 1984), p. 404.

5. Stephen Jay Gould, "Nonmoral Nature," in *A World of Ideas*, ed. Lee A. Jacobus (Boston: Bedford Books, 1994), p. 469.

6. Ibid., p. 472.

7. Peter Irons, *The Courage of Their Convictions: Sixteen Americans Who Fought Their Way to the Supreme Court* (New York: Free Press/Macmillan, 1988), p. 210.

8. Ibid.

9. *Epperson v. Arkansas*, (Supreme Court of the United States, Oral Arguments, No. 7, 1968), p. 7.

10. Ibid., p. 8.

Chapter 3. On the Road to the Supreme Court

1. John Keienburg, "*Epperson v. Arkansas*: A Question of Control Over Curriculum and Instruction Decision Making in the Public Schools," (dissertation, Texas A&M University, 1978), p. 24.

2. Ibid., p. 20.

3. Ibid., p. 24.

4. "Monkey Law Principal Defends Individual Rights," *Arkansas Gazette*, October 16, 1965, p. 1.

5. Keienburg, p. 26.

6. Jennifer Davis, "Education," in *American Decades: 1950–1959*, ed. Richard Layman (Detroit: Gale Research, Inc., 1994), pp. 124–126.

7. Peter Irons, *The Courage of Their Convictions: Sixteen Americans Who Fought Their Way to the Supreme Court* (New York: Free Press/Macmillan, 1988), p. 209.

8. Keienburg, p. 36.

9. Ibid., p. 44.

10. Edward J. Larson, *Trial and Error: The American Controversy over Creation and Evolution* (New York: Oxford University Press, 1985), p. 98.

11. Ibid.

12. David Hill, "Counter Evolutionary," *Teacher Magazine*, November/December 1996, p. 24.

13. Keienburg, p. 43.

14. Irons, p. 221.

15. Susan Epperson, "Teaching in the Bible Belt," in *Irons*, p. 223.

16. Keienburg, p. 51.

17. Ibid., p. 54.

18. Ibid., p. 57.

19. *Epperson* v. *Arkansas* (Supreme Court of the United States, Oral Arguments, No. 7, 1968), p. 11.

20. Irons, p. 212.

21. Keienburg, p. 70.

22. Irons, p. 212.

23. Larson, p. 99.

24. Irons, p. 213.

25. Ibid.

Chapter 4. Susan Epperson Goes to the Supreme Court

1. Joe McGinniss, *The Last Brother* (New York: Simon & Schuster, 1993), pp. 497–498.

2. Susanna McBee and John Neary, "Evolution Revolution in Arkansas," *Life*, November 22, 1968, p. 89.

3. *Epperson* v. *Arkansas* (Supreme Court of the United States, Oral Arguments, No. 7, 1968), p. 3.

4. Ibid., p. 4.

5. Ibid., p. 6.

6. Ibid.

7. Scott Derks, ed., *The Value of a Dollar: Prices and Incomes in the United States, 1860–1989* (Detroit: Gale Research, Inc., 1994), pp. 205, 441.

8. *Epperson* v. *Arkansas* (Oral Arguments), p. 7.

9. Ibid., p. 8.

10. Ibid., p. 9.

Chapter 5. Arkansas Responds to Epperson's Lawsuit

1. *Epperson* v. *Arkansas* (Supreme Court of the United States, Oral Arguments, No. 7, 1968), pp. 9–10.

2. Ibid., p. 10.

3. Fred P. Graham, "Darwin and That Theory Are Back in Court," *The New York Times*, October 17, 1968, p. 45.

4. *Epperson* v. *Arkansas*, (Oral Arguments), p. 10.

5. Ibid., p. 11.

6. Ibid., p. 12.

7. *Epperson* v. *Arkansas* (Supreme Court of the United Sates Decision, No. 7, 1968), p. 3.

8. *Epperson* v. *Arkansas* (Oral Arguments), p. 13.

9. Ibid., p. 15.

10. Ibid.

11. Ibid., p. 16.

12. Ibid., p. 17.

13. Ibid., p. 19.

Chapter 6. *Epperson* v. *Arkansas* Reaches a Conclusion

1. Bernard Schwartz, *A History of the Supreme Court* (New York: Oxford University Press, 1993), p. 263.

2. Ibid., p. 264.

3. Ibid., p. 277.

4. Robert J. Wagman, *The Supreme Court: A Citizen's Guide* (New York: Pharos Books, 1993), pp. 107–113.

5. Kermit L. Hall, ed., *The Oxford Companion to the Supreme Court of the United States* (New York: Oxford University Press, 1992), p. 263.

6. Ibid., pp. 536–537.

7. Ibid., pp. 484–485.

8. Peter Irons, *The Courage of Their Convictions: Sixteen Americans Who Fought Their Way to the Supreme Court* (New York: Free Press/Macmillan, 1988), p. 214.

9. *Epperson* v. *Arkansas* (Supreme Court of the United States Decision, No. 7, 1968), p. 4.

10. Ibid., p. 4.

11. Ibid., p. 2.

12. Ed Johnson, "Arkansas Law on Evolution Struck Down: It Violates Amendments, Justices Say," *Arkansas Gazette*, November 13, 1968, p. 2A.

13. *Epperson* v. *Arkansas* (Decision), p. 4.

14. Ibid., p. 10.

15. Ibid., p. 13.

16. Ibid., p. 14.

17. John Keienburg, "*Epperson* v. *Arkansas*: A Question of Control Over Curriculum and Instruction Decision Making in the Public Schools" (dissertation, Texas A&M University, 1978), p. 114.

18. "'Clear Conscience' Is Seen for State Biology Teachers," *Arkansas Gazette*, November 13, 1968, p. 1A.

19. L. Sprague DeCamp, "The End of the Monkey War," *Scientific American*, February 1969, pp. 15–21.

20. "Scopes Elated, but Warns 'The Fight Will Still Go On,'" *Arkansas Gazette*, November 13, 1968, p. 1A.

21. "Law Was Ignored, Schoolmen Contend: They Won't Miss It," *Arkansas Gazette*, November 13, 1968, p. 1A.

22. Ibid.

23. Ibid.

Chapter 7. Where Do We Go After *Epperson*?

1. Christopher P. Toumey, *God's Own Scientists: Creationists in a Secular World* (New Brunswick, N.J.: Rutgers University Press, 1994), p. 35.

2. Ibid., p. 36.

3. Ibid., p. 49.

4. Ibid., p. 37.

5. Ibid., p. 38.

6. Ibid., p. 39.

7. David Hill, "Counter Evolutionary," *Teacher Magazine*, November/December 1996, p. 24.

8. Toumey, pp. 46–47.

9. Hill, p. 25.

10. Ibid.

11. Ibid.

12. Ibid.

13. Toumey, p. 49.

Glossary

appeal—A request for a new hearing of a court case, transferring the case from a lower court to a higher court.

atheist—A person who does not believe in the existence of any god, divine authority, or higher power.

bailiff—A court official who maintains order and escorts witnesses in and out of the courtroom.

chancery court—Originally a British term for one of the five divisions of the British High Court of Justice. It is used in Arkansas to mean a local, county court.

Church of England—The national church of Great Britain with its home base in Canterbury, England.

communism—A political and economic system under which there is no private property and workers are organized for the good of the nation. Before 1990, the most powerful Communist nation was the U.S.S.R., or the Soviet Union.

concurring opinion—A legal agreement written by a judge who agrees with the court's decision but disagrees with the reasoning used to arrive at the decision.

creationism—A belief in the biblical, Christian account of how God created the universe and all of its living things.

creation scientist—A Christian who uses the methods of modern science to verify religious truths of the Bible.

defendant—The person, organization, state, or nation against whom a legal action is taken. The defendant in *Epperson* v. *Arkansas* was the state of Arkansas.

evolution—Charles Darwin's theory that living creatures change over time due to their interactions with the environment, as a result of natural selection.

fundamentalist—A person who believes in a literal, strict interpretation of the Bible and who upholds the Bible's basic, fundamental truths.

integration—Providing people of different racial and ethnic groups equal, unrestricted use of public resources such as housing, schools, hospitals, and businesses.

natural selection—Charles Darwin's theory that nature works through a process by which animals and plants adapt to their environment.

per curiam—An order by a higher court overturning the decision of a lower court without providing explicit reasoning.

plaintiff—The person who is named first and initiates a lawsuit.

precedent—The previous court cases related to the current case before a court. The court should decide the case before it by using legal reasoning consistent with previous decisions.

segregation—The process of separating different racial and ethnic groups to prevent them from participating together in schools, jobs, housing, and other aspects of public life.

Further Reading

Bantock, Cuillin. *The Story of Life.* New York: Peter Benick Books, 1984.

Corrick, James A. *Recent Revolutions in Biology.* New York: Franklin Watts, 1987.

Coville, Bruce. *Prehistoric People.* New York: Doubleday, 1990.

Ditfurth, Hoimar von. *Origins of Life: Evolution as Creation,* trans. Peter Heinegg. San Francisco: Harper & Row, 1982.

Eve, Raymond A., and Francis B. Harrold. *The Creationist Movement in Modern America.* Boston: Twayne, 1991.

Fisher, Maxine P. Recent *Revolutions in Anthropology.* New York: Franklin Watts, 1986.

Irons, Peter, and Stephanie Guitton, eds. *May It Please the Court: 23 Live Recordings of Landmark Cases As Argued Before the Supreme Court.* New York: New Press, 1993.

Kitcher, Philip. *Abusing Science: The Case Against Creationism.* Cambridge: Massachusetts Institute of Technology Press, 1982.

Larson, Edward J. *Trial and Error: The American Controversy Over Creation and Evolution.* New York: Oxford University Press, 1985.

Lasky, Kathryn. *Traces of Life: The Origins of Humankind.* New York: Morrow Junior Books, 1989.

Leaky, Richard E. *Human Origins.* New York: Lodestar Books, 1982.

Matthews, Rupert. *The First People.* New York: Bookwright, 1990.

McCollister, Betty, ed. *Voices for Evolution.* Berkeley, Calif.: National Center for Science Education, 1989.

Montagu, Ashley, ed. *Science and Creationism.* New York: Oxford University Press, 1984.

Numbers, Ronald L. *The Creationists.* New York: A. A. Knopf, 1992.

Taylor, Ron. *The Story of Evolution.* New York: Warwick Press, 1981.

Wills, Gary. *Under God: Religion and American Politics.* New York: Simon & Schuster, 1990.

Internet Sites

Creationism
<http://www.leepfrog.com/~johnjo/creation.htm>

Creationism and Creation Science
<http://dcn.davis.ca.us/~btcarrol/skeptic/creation.html>

Darwin and Evolution Overview
<http://www.stg.brown.edu/projects/hypertext//landow/ victorian/darwin/darwinov.html>

Evolution
<http://www.students.uiuc.edu/~aronoff/Evolution.html>

Science versus Creationism
<http://alice.uoregon.edu/~mark/create.html>

Index

127

128